Machine Learning System Design Interview

3 Books in 1: The Ultimate Guide to Master System Design and Machine Learning Interviews—From Beginners to Advanced Techniques

Mark Reed & CyberPress Edge

© Copyright 2024 - All rights reserved.

The content contained within this book may not be reproduced, duplicated or transmitted without direct written permission from the author or the publisher.

Under no circumstances will any blame or legal responsibility be held against the publisher, or author, for any damages, reparation, or monetary loss due to the information contained within this book, either directly or indirectly.

Legal Notice:

This book is copyright protected. It is only for personal use. You cannot amend, distribute, sell, use, quote or paraphrase any part, or the content within this book, without the consent of the author or publisher.

Disclaimer Notice:

Please note the information contained within this document is for educational and entertainment purposes only. All effort has been executed to present accurate, up to date, reliable, complete information. No warranties of any kind are declared or implied. Readers acknowledge that the author is not engaged in the rendering of legal, financial, medical or professional advice. The content within this book has been derived from various sources. Please consult a licensed professional before attempting any techniques outlined in this book.

By reading this document, the reader agrees that under no circumstances is the author responsible for any losses, direct or indirect, that are incurred as a result of the use of the information contained within this document, including, but not limited to, errors, omissions, or inaccuracies.

Table for Contents

INTRODUCTION v

BOOK 1: FOUNDATIONS OF MACHINE LEARNING SYSTEM DESIGN ... ix

- **Chapter 1:** Introduction to Machine Learning System Design 1
- **Chapter 2:** Core Machine Learning Concepts 10
- **Chapter 3:** Fundamental System Design Principles 20
- **Chapter 4:** Machine Learning Lifecycle 26
- **Chapter 5:** Basic ML System Architectures.. 32
- **Chapter 6:** Data Management for ML Systems 39
- **Chapter 7:** Model Training and Optimization 46
- **Chapter 8:** ML Model Deployment Strategies 56

BOOK 2: ADVANCED MACHINE LEARNING SYSTEM DESIGN 65

- **Chapter 9:** Deep Learning Systems... 67
- **Chapter 10:** Natural Language Processing Systems.. 76
- **Chapter 11:** Computer Vision Systems 86
- **Chapter 12:** Recommender Systems.. 95
- **Chapter 13:** Time Series and Anomaly Detection 105
- **Chapter 14:** Reinforcement Learning Systems 115
- **Chapter 15:** MLOps and Continuous Delivery for ML 124

BOOK 3: MASTERING THE ML SYSTEM DESIGN INTERVIEW 135

- **Chapter 15:** Interview Preparation Strategies 137
- **Chapter 17:** Problem-Solving Framework... 153
- **Chapter 18:** Case Studies and Practice Problems.. 169
- **Chapter 19:** Advanced Interview Techniques 185
- **Chapter 20:** Final Preparation and Future Trends 195

GLOSSARY 212

REFERENCES 217

Introduction

In today's world, where advancements occur at lightning speed. One particular skill is becoming a crucial differentiator for those aiming to carve out a niche in the tech landscape: mastering machine learning (ML) system design. Imagine standing on the cusp of an era defined by intelligent systems capable of processing vast amounts of data and generating transformative insights. For software engineers contemplating a leap into the burgeoning field of ML, understanding the intricacies of system design is quite beneficial. If you're looking to make that transition, or if you're already immersed in the world of ML but seek to fortify your expertise, this book is meticulously crafted just for you.

ML, often heralded as the frontier of modern-day innovation, holds boundless potential for software engineers, data scientists, and academic hopefuls alike. Yet, the journey from proficiency in conventional software roles to mastery in machine learning requires more than just a basic understanding of algorithms and models. It demands a comprehensive grasp of how these models integrate into larger systems, addressing the unique challenges and considerations of scalability, reliability, and performance. What this book offers is an all-encompassing guide that bridges this gap. Through its pages, you will traverse the rich landscape of ML system design, converging multiple facets into a singular, powerful resource.

This book is for a diverse yet interconnected audience, each poised at different stages of their career paths but unified by a common goal: Excellence in ML. Are you a software engineer who has honed your skills in coding and development? You likely understand the nuances of creating robust applications, but now you stand at the threshold of something altogether new. Here, you'll find guidance on translating your existing knowledge into this specialized domain. For data scientists and ML engineers eyeing positions at top-tier tech firms, success lies in the intersection of technical competence and articulate communication. This book helps you with both, marrying foundational principles with practical insights that prepare you for rigorous interview processes. And if you're a graduate or student, brimming with enthusiasm yet seeking direction in ML careers, consider this your roadmap to industry-standard practices and formats, laying down a robust foundation for your ambitions.

In an age where competition is fierce, and opportunities abound, what sets you apart is not just the ability to develop ML models but the capacity to envision and articulate their integration into broader systems. What does mastering ML system design mean for you? It means having the confidence to step into any interview room and converse fluently about intricate system architectures. It's the empowerment of knowing that you can contribute meaningfully to the technological narratives unfolding within leading enterprises. Most profoundly, mastering this discipline transforms you from a participant in tech evolution to a pioneer, shaping the future of intelligent systems.

Throughout this book, expect to be guided through content designed to explore the complexities of ML system design. With every chapter, you'll gain insights that not only improve your technical acumen but also refine the way you convey complex ideas succinctly and effectively. Whether you're solving real-world problems or showcasing your thought process in high-pressure interview settings, the skills acquired here will prove indispensable.

This book is also constructed with a modern reader in mind. Gone are the days of wading through dense jargon and impenetrable prose. Instead, anticipate clear, approachable language that resonates with today's tech enthusiasts. Dive into descriptive narratives that illuminate concepts rather than obscure them. The informal tone pervading our discussions ensures that learning feels less like a chore and more like an engaging dialogue between peers.

This book has a simple goal: To provide you with the information and abilities needed to effectively approach ML system design interviews. Whether you're looking for positions at top-tier tech firms or preparing for interviews at developing startups, this book can help you with the following:

- **Understand Key Concepts:** Gain a deep understanding of ML system design fundamentals, from scalability to real-time processing and fault tolerance.

- **Develop Practical Skills:** Learn how to apply theoretical knowledge to real-world scenarios with practical exercises and case studies.

- **Master Interview Techniques:** Prepare for common interview questions and challenges related to ML systems, and practice articulating your thought process in a structured, clear manner.

- **Build Confidence:** Learn how to navigate high-pressure interview settings, showcasing your ability to design efficient, scalable ML systems.

By the end, not only will you possess a reinforced knowledge of system design for ML, but you'll also have developed a nuanced understanding of your role within this dynamic field. As you turn the final pages, it is our hope that you will be not just a more informed individual but a confident practitioner ready to seize the myriad opportunities awaiting in the tech universe.

Ultimately, this book isn't just about acquiring knowledge; it's about transformation. It's about giving you the tools to ascend to new professional heights and encouraging you to become an ambassador of change within the ML community. So gear up to embark on this exciting journey—a journey toward mastering machine learning system design and unlocking the doors to a future teeming with possibilities. Welcome aboard!

BOOK 1

Foundations of Machine Learning System Design

CHAPTER 1

Introduction to Machine Learning System Design

Designing a ML system is like crafting an intricate puzzle, where each piece must fit seamlessly to unlock the full potential of AI. This captivating process blends creativity with precision and offers a playground for those eager to explore the interplay between theory and real-world application. Picture the journey of transforming complex algorithms into practical solutions that can be scaled and refined to meet dynamic demands. For aspiring ML engineers and software enthusiasts transitioning into this field, understanding system design is about knowing the mechanics as well as envisioning how these systems come alive in everyday scenarios.

This chapter goes into a fascinating exploration of the core elements that constitute effective ML system design. It explores the essence of why thoughtful planning and execution are critical for achieving efficient, scalable, and meaningful outcomes. You'll discover how good design can enhance model efficiency, making them faster and more precise while also ensuring scalability to accommodate growing data volumes. The chapter further uncovers the alignment of ML outputs with real-world applications, highlighting the need for systems that generate actionable insights across various industries. As we go deeper into the subject, you'll gain insight into the essential components and skills needed for building these systems, providing a solid framework for anyone preparing for technical interviews or aiming to excel in the world of ML.

Definition and Importance of ML System Design

ML system design is like constructing the blueprint of a building before the bricks are laid. It forms the structured framework necessary to turn theoretical AI concepts into tangible solutions. Imagine you're building sophisticated machinery—it won't operate without a well-thought-out structure that ensures every part functions in harmony. This analogy applies to deploying ML models; system design is about integrating these models effectively within larger systems. The process involves considering how data flows through the model, how predictions are generated, and how those predictions interact with other components. For professionals transitioning into ML roles or preparing for interviews, understanding this facet is vital, as it demonstrates one's ability to think beyond algorithms to full-fledged systems.

The Impact of Good System Design on Model Performance

The benefits of effective system design span across various dimensions, but improving model efficiency stands out as fundamental. Good system design can lead to faster processing times and more accurate predictions, two elements crucial in environments where time and precision are of the essence. For instance, consider a real-time fraud detection system used by banks. An efficiently designed system allows for those fraudulent transactions to be flagged instantly, saving potential losses. When optimized resources are allocated and used, design practices can drastically minimize latency and computational overhead, leading to swift decision-making processes. In an interview setting, articulating how you can enhance model efficiency through thoughtful design might just set you apart from other candidates.

Scalability When Designing ML Systems

Scalability is another critical consideration when designing ML systems. As companies grow, so does their data, sometimes exponentially. A well-designed system can handle increasing volumes of data and users gracefully, making sure there's consistent performance. Consider Netflix's recommendation engine, which needs to provide personalized content suggestions that meet each user's preferences. With millions of subscribers worldwide, scalability is not just a luxury; it's a necessity. The system must manage to deliver quick recommendations regardless of user load. Software engineers eyeing a shift toward ML system design need to anticipate such demands and make sure that designs accommodate future growth without necessitating major overhauls.

Aligning ML outputs with real-world applications is important in system design. It's not enough for a model to produce results; those results need to be meaningful and applicable to everyday scenarios. Take autonomous vehicles that rely heavily on ML. If a self-driving car's system isn't designed to interpret its environment accurately while accounting for human safety, then its usefulness diminishes significantly. Effective system design ensures that outputs are relevant and actionable, maintaining alignment with user needs and practical constraints.

Practical Example

For example, in healthcare, ML models can predict patient outcomes, potentially revolutionizing treatment plans and resource allocation. However, the outputs are only valuable if integrated within systems that doctors and healthcare providers find easy to use and reliable. Systems should be intuitive, providing clear insights without overwhelming users with unnecessary technical details. Designers should prioritize user experience, knowing that information flows seamlessly from model insights to actionable steps. The capacity to present models' capabilities clearly and contextually in real-world scenarios is invaluable, especially during interviews where demonstrating practical knowledge reflects readiness for job responsibilities.

Components of an ML System

Understanding the integral components of a ML system is foundational for anyone stepping into this field, especially if you're preparing for technical interviews. Let's dive right into these key elements, starting with data ingestion and preprocessing pipelines.

Data Ingestion and Preprocessing Pipelines

The first step in any ML project involves dealing with data, the lifeblood of your model. Think of data ingestion as the process by which raw data is collected from various sources, whether it's databases, logs, sensors, or online repositories. But raw data isn't typically useful out of the gate—it needs to be refined through preprocessing pipelines. These pipelines are crucial because they cleanse and transform the data into formats that models can understand and learn from effectively. For instance, noisy or missing data can lead to inaccurate models, so preprocessing might involve filling in missing values, removing duplicates, or normalizing numerical features. This stage ensures that your data is robust and ready for further use, setting a solid foundation for model training.

Feature Engineering and Selection Process

Once your data is prepared, the next focus is on feature engineering and selection processes. In the simplest terms, feature engineering is about creating new input variables from your existing data set to improve model performance. It's like enhancing ingredients before cooking a meal. If your dataset includes timestamps, you might extract features like "hour of day" or "day of the week" to find patterns not initially visible. Also, feature selection hones in on choosing the most relevant data features, ensuring that the model isn't overwhelmed by noise. Employing techniques such as correlation matrices or LASSO regression helps identify these critical features. The goal here is optimization: By selecting the right features, you increase model efficiency and accuracy while reducing computational costs.

Model Training and Evaluation

Model training and evaluation come next. After deciding which features to use, it's time to train your model using them. This phase involves feeding data into a learning algorithm so it can recognize patterns and make decisions or predictions based on new data. A significant part of model training is selecting the right algorithm, whether it's decision trees, support vector machines, or neural networks, depending on the problem at hand. Evaluation, on the other hand, measures how well your trained model performs on unseen data. Techniques such as cross-validation ensure that your model's predictions are not only accurate but also generalize well across different datasets. Improving model accuracy often involves tweaking hyperparameters or adopting ensemble methods like boosting or bagging. Additionally, avoiding overfitting is critical, which happens when a model performs well on training data but poorly on new data; regularization techniques or dropout in neural networks can help address this issue.

The Different Deployment Techniques

Finally, let's discuss deployment techniques, an often overlooked yet vital component of ML systems. Once a model is fine-tuned and ready, it must move from a controlled development environment to real-world production settings, where it starts making actual predictions. This transition requires careful planning to allow seamless integration with existing systems. Deployment may involve containerization tools like Docker, which encapsulate everything needed to run the model, ensuring consistency across various environments. Additionally, platforms like Kubernetes manage these containers for scalability and reliability. Monitoring and maintaining the deployed model is important, allowing for timely updates as new data comes in or as circumstances change. Implementing CI/CD (continuous integration/continuous deployment) practices can automate model updates, ensuring minimal downtime and consistent performance.

Overview of Technical Interviews for ML Roles

Technical interviews for ML roles, particularly those focusing on system design, typically follow a structured format designed to assess a candidate's technical knowledge, problem-solving skills, and ability to design scalable ML systems. These interviews often consist of multiple rounds, each with a specific focus.

The initial round usually begins a phone or video screening, where candidates are asked basic technical questions to know their fundamental understanding of ML concepts and system design principles. This screening helps companies filter candidates and determine if they're ready for more in-depth technical assessments.

Following the initial screening, candidates often face one or more rounds of technical interviews. These may include coding interviews, where candidates are asked to solve algorithmic problems or implement ML algorithms. While coding skills are important, the emphasis in ML system design interviews is typically on high-level design and architecture rather than low-level implementation details.

The core of the ML system design interview usually encompasses one or more system design questions. In these sessions, candidates are presented with a complex problem, such as designing a recommendation system for an e-commerce platform or creating a real-time fraud detection system for a financial institution. Candidates are expected to walk through their thought process, discussing various components of the system, data flow, model selection, and scalability considerations.

Some companies also incorporate case study interviews, where candidates are given a real-world scenario and asked to analyze it from a ML perspective. This might mean discussing how to approach a particular business problem using ML, considering factors like data availability, model selection, and potential challenges in implementation.

Behavior Interviews and How to Overcome Them

Behavioral interviews are often part of the process as well. While not strictly technical, these interviews assess a candidate's soft skills, past experiences, and ability to work in a team environment, which are all crucial factors in successfully designing and implementing ML systems in real-world settings. Many top tech companies have adopted the concept of "loop" interviews, where candidates meet with several team members in succession, each focusing on different aspects of ML system design. This approach provides a comprehensive evaluation of the candidate's skills and allows the candidate to interact with potential future colleagues.

It's worth noting that some companies have started incorporating practical assignments into their interview process. These might involve take-home projects where candidates are asked to design a small ML system or solve a specific problem, providing a more realistic assessment of their skills. Understanding these various interview formats and being prepared for each type is absolutely essential for success in ML system design interviews. As we progress through this book, we'll go deeper into strategies for excelling in each of these interview scenarios, providing you with the tools and knowledge to confidently navigate the ML system design interview process.

Skills and Tools Required for ML Roles

When preparing for ML interviews, it's important to possess a variety of skills and tools. Among these, proficiency in programming languages like Python and Java is indispensable. Python is celebrated for its simplicity and extensive libraries like NumPy and Pandas, which are often used in data manipulation and analysis—a fundamental precursor to model building. Similarly, Python's scikit-learn library offers powerful features for implementing a wide range of ML algorithms, making it an excellent choice for both beginners and seasoned professionals.

Great Examples of Skills to Work On

Let me give you some great skills that will definitely help you:

Java: Java, on the other hand, shines in large-scale enterprise environments. Its strong typing system and performance efficiency make it particularly suitable for developing complex, scalable applications. Many enterprises rely on Java-based ecosystems, which requires familiarity with this language for individuals aiming to work within such organizations. A deep understanding of these programming languages not only enhances your ability to construct robust ML models but also arms you with the tools needed to implement efficient solutions during technical assessments.

TensorFlow: In parallel, gaining expertise in frameworks like TensorFlow and PyTorch can significantly accelerate your journey into ML. These frameworks are essential tools in building and deploying models efficiently. TensorFlow, developed by Google, provides a comprehensive ecosystem for end-to-end model deployment. It supports deep learning models with capabilities for refining model parameters through backpropagation and gradient descent techniques. This makes it highly versatile across different ML tasks.

PyTorch: PyTorch, favored for its dynamic computational graph, offers flexibility and ease of experimentation. It's particularly useful for researchers and developers who value a more interactive environment where the graph structure can be modified on the fly. Both frameworks come with their own sets of community resources, tutorials, and pre-trained models, which make them user-friendly and accessible. Mastery of these tools allows you to seamlessly translate theoretical knowledge into practical application, a vital asset during interview evaluations.

Understanding of Distributed Systems and Cloud Computing Platforms

Another key skill area is understanding distributed systems and cloud computing platforms. As ML models and datasets grow in complexity and size, leveraging distributed systems becomes increasingly important. Platforms like Apache Spark provide the ability to process data in parallel, thus reducing computation time and enhancing efficiency. Cloud services from providers like AWS, Google Cloud, and Azure offer scalable infrastructure to deploy ML models at scale. Familiarity with these technologies allows candidates to discuss and handle real-world challenges during interviews, such as optimizing resource allocation or implementing scalable architectures.

Cloud-based tools like AWS SageMaker or Google AI Platform enable faster prototyping and deployment of ML models. They integrate seamlessly with other cloud services, providing end-to-end solutions from data ingestion to production deployment. Demonstrating expertise in these areas signals to potential employers that you are capable of managing complex ML workflows, which is often a requirement for advanced roles.

Common Technical Interview Formats and Coding Challenges

Also, familiarizing yourself with common technical interview formats can give you a strategic edge. ML interviews may encompass algorithmic questions, coding challenges, and case studies. These formats aim to assess your problem-solving skills, coding proficiency, and ability to apply ML concepts effectively. Preparing for algorithmic questions typically involves practicing data structures and algorithms, commonly tested through platforms like LeetCode or HackerRank.

Coding challenges, on the other hand, require fluency in writing clean, efficient code under time constraints. Engaging in mock interviews or coding sessions can help improve your speed and accuracy, which are critical factors in these assessments. Additionally, many ML interviews incorporate case studies where candidates must solve real-world problems using ML methodologies. Here, showcasing your thought process and explaining your decisions clearly is just as important as deriving the correct solution.

When you focus on articulating your problem-solving approach, whether it's selecting suitable models based on given data or evaluating trade-offs between different algorithms, you're able to demonstrate a well-rounded understanding of ML principles. This approach helps in cracking interviews and reinforces your grasp over fundamental concepts, enabling you to stand out among peers.

Quizzes and Exercises

Quiz

1. What is machine learning system design, and why is it important in AI applications?

2. How does good system design impact model performance and scalability?

3. Name and briefly describe three key components of a typical ML system.

4. What are the most common interview formats for ML system design positions?

5. List three essential programming languages or frameworks commonly used in ML system design.

Exercises

1. **Conceptual Design Exercise:** Sketch a high-level design for a basic ML system that could be used for sentiment analysis of social media posts. Include key components such as data ingestion, preprocessing, feature engineering, model training, and inference. Explain the role of each component in your design.

2. **Tool Exploration:** Choose one ML framework (e.g., TensorFlow, PyTorch, or scikit-learn) and one cloud computing platform (e.g., AWS, Google Cloud, or Azure). Research and write a brief summary (250–300 words) of how these tools can be used together in ML system design. Focus on their strengths and any potential limitations.

3. **Interview Preparation:** Say you're preparing for an ML system design interview. Create a checklist of 5–7 key points you would want to cover when explaining your approach to designing an ML system. For each point, write a brief explanation of why it's important.

Key Insights and Practical Takeaways

- **System Design Foundation:** Approach ML system design as crafting a blueprint before implementation. Ensure a structured framework that integrates theoretical AI concepts into practical, scalable solutions.

- **Performance Optimization:** Focus on designing systems that enhance model efficiency, leading to faster processing times and more accurate predictions. This is crucial for real-time applications like fraud detection systems.

- **Scalability Planning:** Anticipate future growth in data volume and user base. Design systems that can handle increasing demands gracefully, similar to Netflix's recommendation engine that serves millions of users.

- **Data Pipeline Management:** Prioritize robust data ingestion and preprocessing pipelines. These are foundational for cleaning and transforming raw data into formats suitable for model training and analysis.

- **Feature Engineering:** Invest time in creating and selecting the most relevant features. This process can significantly improve model performance and efficiency while reducing computational costs.

- **Model Training and Evaluation:** Choose appropriate algorithms and evaluation techniques based on your specific problem. Implement strategies like cross-validation and regularization to ensure model generalization and prevent overfitting.

- **Deployment Strategies:** Familiarize yourself with containerization tools like Docker and orchestration platforms like Kubernetes for seamless model deployment and scaling in production environments.

- **Continuous Learning:** Stay updated with ML frameworks like TensorFlow and PyTorch, as well as cloud platforms such as AWS SageMaker or Google AI Platform, for efficient model development and deployment.

CHAPTER 2

Core Machine Learning Concepts

ML is like opening a door to a world where computers learn from data and make decisions without explicit instructions. Instead of hardcoding specifics, these intelligent systems extract patterns and insights from the information they process. This chapter dives into the core concepts that drive this fascinating domain, offering a glimpse into the primary learning paradigms and their important roles in technology today. Just picture machines that evolve through experience just as humans do—learning from examples, making predictions, and offering solutions to complex problems. It's an exhilarating journey into how algorithms can achieve what once seemed reserved for human intellect.

This is what we will be looking at in this chapter. More specifically, the intriguing division between supervised and unsupervised learning, illustrating how each serves distinct purposes in ML endeavors. With supervised learning, you'll discover how labeled datasets steer models toward accurate predictions, much like a guided tour with clear directions. Meanwhile, the allure of unsupervised learning lies in its ability to uncover hidden structures within data, such as wandering through uncharted territory to find unknown treasures. Beyond these foundations, the chapter unfolds into semi-supervised and reinforcement learning techniques, bridging gaps between labeled and unlabeled frameworks and venturing into realms of feedback-driven intelligence. As we journey further, we'll look into algorithm types like classification, regression, and clustering, which are essential tools that shape the landscape of ML. This chapter is a gateway to understanding these foundational pillars, setting the stage for practical applications and deeper insights in the vast field of artificial intelligence.

Learning Paradigms: Supervised vs. Unsupervised

ML, with its diverse array of techniques and methods, often begins with an understanding of the foundational paradigms: supervised and unsupervised learning. These paradigms are essential to understand as they establish the core framework through which many ML systems operate. At the heart of these paradigms are fundamental differences in data usage and the types of problems they address.

Definitions and Key Differences Between Supervised and Unsupervised Learning

It's important that you understand the main differences between supervised and unsupervised learning, as this will often be common in the ML space.

Supervised Learning

Supervised learning, as the name suggests, involves guidance from labeled data. Imagine a teacher guiding a student through a series of exercises where each question comes with the correct answer; this is like how supervised learning functions. Algorithms in this category rely on labeled datasets to learn patterns and predict outcomes for tasks like classification and regression. Think of a spam detection system analyzing emails: it's trained on a dataset where each email is already labeled as "spam" or "not spam." Over time, the algorithm learns the little things that differentiate legitimate messages from unwanted ones, becoming adept at identifying spam based on learned patterns.

Unsupervised Learning

On the other hand, unsupervised learning operates without the luxury of labeled data. It's like exploring a new city without a map, relying solely on senses and intuition to navigate. In this paradigm, algorithms attempt to identify hidden structures within the data. This approach suits tasks such as clustering and dimensionality reduction. Consider customer segmentation in marketing: Companies might not have prior labels indicating specific segments within their customer base. Through unsupervised learning, algorithms can analyze purchasing behaviors and interaction patterns, emerging with distinct customer groups that enable more tailored marketing strategies.

Despite being distinct, supervised and unsupervised learning share common ground in their goal to extract meaningful insights from data. Often, real-world scenarios aren't confined neatly within the boundaries of one paradigm. This is where semi-supervised and reinforcement learning come into play, bridging gaps between purely labeled or unlabeled frameworks.

Semi-Supervised and Reinforcement Learning: Bridging the Gap

Semi-supervised learning exists as a hybrid approach. This technique leverages both labeled and unlabeled data. It's like having a blend of guided practice and exploratory learning, drawing strengths from both. This method becomes particularly advantageous when acquiring labeled data, which is costly or labor-intensive, yet there's an abundance of unlabeled data readily available. A practical example would be image recognition in medical diagnostics, where only a portion of images may be expertly annotated, and the rest remain unlabeled.

Reinforcement learning further broadens the horizon by integrating feedback mechanisms as part of its learning process. To give you an example, picture a robot navigating a maze: It receives feedback in the form of rewards or penalties based on its actions. The ultimate aim is for the robot to maximize cumulative rewards, gradually discovering the most efficient path through trial and error. Reinforcement learning shines in domains requiring decision-making and strategy development, such as game-playing AI or autonomous driving systems.

Real-World Applications and Use Cases for Each Learning Paradigm

Practical applications of these paradigms highlight their relevance across diverse fields. Supervised learning's applicability extends far beyond spam detection to encompass industries like sentiment analysis, where it deciphers emotions conveyed in text data, and fraud detection systems in finance, meticulously scrutinizing transactions to uncover anomalies. Unsupervised learning finds its niche in anomaly detection, unveiling rare events against a backdrop of normal behavior, which is important in network security or equipment maintenance.

Customer segmentation exemplifies unsupervised learning, empowering businesses to personalize experiences and optimize engagement strategies without prior assumptions. It paves the way for targeted advertising, loyalty programs, and product development, ultimately enhancing customer satisfaction and business performance.

Algorithm Types: Classification, Regression, and Clustering

ML is a rapidly expanding field, and understanding the main types of algorithms involved is essential for anyone aspiring to make a mark in this area. Essentially, ML is about a variety of techniques and models designed to help computers learn from data and make decisions without being explicitly programmed. The three primary types of algorithms prevalent in ML are classification, regression, and clustering. Each of these has distinct purposes and is relevant in different contexts.

1. Understanding Classification Problems and Algorithms

Classification is one of the most common tasks in ML, involving assigning input data into predefined categories or classes. Classification algorithms are particularly useful when we need to sort items into a limited set of groups based on their features. For instance, logistic regression can be employed to predict binary outcomes, such as determining whether an email is spam or not. Another powerful classification algorithm is the Support Vector Machine (SVM), which works by finding the optimal boundary between the possible outputs, essentially creating the best separation between classes in datasets with many variables. These algorithms are vital in fields ranging from healthcare, for predicting diseases, to finance, to credit scoring.

2. Regression Techniques and Their Applications

Moving on to regression methods, these algorithms are key when it comes to predicting continuous outcomes. Linear regression is a fundamental technique that estimates the relationship between a dependent variable and one or more independent variables by fitting a linear equation to observed data. If you've ever plotted a trend line on a scatter plot, that's essentially linear regression at work. If we extend this concept, polynomial regression can model relationships between variables by considering polynomial functions of the predictors, which allows a more flexible fit for curve-like relationships. These methods are invaluable in scenarios where forecasting and predictions are required, such as estimating home prices based on various factors or predicting stock market trends over time.

3. Clustering Algorithms and Their Use in Unsupervised Learning

Clustering techniques bring us into the world of unsupervised learning, where the task is to group similar data points together without explicit labels. A popular method is K-means clustering, which partitions the dataset into K-clusters with the goal to minimize the distance within each cluster while maximizing the distance between clusters. This is particularly useful in market segmentation, where businesses can identify distinct consumer groups within their customer base. Hierarchical clustering, another technique, builds a tree of clusters that can provide more granular insights into data structure. It's like organizing your files—sometimes, grouping them into folders isn't enough, and you need subfolders to understand the hierarchy better. These clustering techniques are really effective in identifying natural groupings in data, and crucial in applications like image compression and anomaly detection.

Evaluating and Comparing Different Algorithms for Each Type of Problem

When working with these algorithms, choosing the right one for a particular problem is critical. Evaluating and comparing different algorithms allows practitioners to identify the best fit for specific data-driven challenges. Criteria for evaluation could include accuracy, speed, scalability, interpretability, and robustness, among others. For example, while SVMs might perform exceptionally well in cases with clear margin separations, they could falter in extremely large datasets due to computational intensity. On the other hand, logistical regression might be preferred for its simplicity and ease of interpretation, despite potentially lower accuracy compared to other complex models. Additionally, cross-validation techniques play an essential role in assessing how the results of a statistical analysis will generalize to an independent dataset, making sure that models haven't just memorized the data they were trained on.

In practice, choosing and evaluating algorithms is both an art and a science. It's about meticulous testing, experimentation, and often, a deep understanding of the problem domain. Imagine, for instance, a scenario where you're developing a predictive maintenance system for industrial equipment. Initially, you might lean towards regression techniques to estimate failure times, but upon further exploration through clustering, you realize there are underlying operational modes influencing failures that weren't apparent before. Thus, iterative evaluation helps refine assumptions, improve model performance, and ultimately drive successful deployment in real-world settings.

Better Models: Feature Selection and Engineering

Within the world of ML, the importance of choosing the right features has to be highlighted. Strategic feature selection and engineering play an important role in increasing model performance. Essentially, feature selection helps in boosting model accuracy by honing in on the most relevant data attributes. This process is not just about picking random features but involves meticulous methods such as filter, wrapper, and embedded techniques.

Filter Method: The filter method ranks features according to a statistical measure and selects those that are most significant, much like sifting through sand to find golden nuggets. For instance, employing the Chi-squared test or Pearson correlation can help highlight features that have the strongest relationship with the target variable. The advantage here is speed; however, it doesn't account for feature interactions within the model.

Wrapper: This method takes a more holistic approach by using a predictive model to evaluate different subsets of features. Picture trying various ingredient combinations to perfect a recipe. While this method often yields better performance due to its exhaustive search, it's computationally expensive, making it less feasible for large datasets.

Embedded Method: Then there's the embedded method, which combines the best of both worlds by incorporating feature selection within the model training process itself. Techniques like regularization (Lasso, Ridge) are prime examples where unnecessary features are penalized, thus reducing overfitting. This ensures not only efficiency but also a streamlined model development process.

Feature Selection and Engineering

Now, beyond selecting existing features, there exists the art of feature engineering—a task much like creating new ingredients from scratch. This has to do with deriving new, informative features that reveal hidden patterns within the data. Picture transforming raw data into insightful attributes, like converting raw temperature readings into heat indices to better predict energy consumption. Engaging in thoughtful feature transformations, such as encoding categorical variables or scaling numerical ones, can significantly amplify a model's understanding of the data landscape.

Challenges You Might Find

However, there could be challenges when dealing with high-dimensional data. As dimensions increase, the distance between data points swells, leading to sparsity—a phenomenon known as *the curse of dimensionality*. This makes it paramount to mitigate these effects through dimensionality reduction techniques. Principal Component Analysis (PCA), for example, reduces dimensionality by identifying and preserving key components that capture the variance in the data. Visualize it as condensing a lengthy book into a summary without losing its essence.

In a similar way, t-Distributed Stochastic Neighbor Embedding (t-SNE) works wonders for visualizing complex, high-dimensional data in two or three dimensions, thereby uncovering clusters and patterns invisible to the naked eye. Such practices allow for models to not only become more efficient but also less prone to noise and overfitting.

Executing feature selection and engineering effectively leads to streamlined models that boast improved predictive capabilities. With fewer, but more meaningful, features, models train faster and require less computational power. Also, they generalize better on unseen data, proving their worth time and again across various applications.

Real-World Example

Consider a real-world scenario like credit scoring, where ML models determine the likelihood of loan default. When carefully selecting the most impactful features, like payment history and credit utilization, and engineering new ones, such as debt-to-income ratios, the model becomes robust in predicting outcomes, ensuring minimal risk for financial institutions.

As software engineers transition into ML roles, understanding these principles is very important. They offer practical insights into real-world use cases that align seamlessly with system design considerations—an asset during technical interviews at top tech companies. Similarly, for graduates aiming to break into ML careers, mastering these industry-standard practices equips them with the confidence to navigate complex datasets and articulate their thought processes effectively.

Real-World Applications of ML

To illustrate the practical impact of machine learning concepts, let's have a look at several case studies across different industries:

Healthcare—Predictive Diagnostics: A leading hospital implemented a ML system to predict the likelihood of readmissions for patients with chronic diseases. Using supervised learning techniques, the system analyzed patient data, including medical history, current symptoms, and lifestyle factors. The model, based on a random forest algorithm, achieved an accuracy of 85% in predicting readmissions within 30 days of discharge. This allowed healthcare providers to intervene proactively, reducing readmission rates by 23% over a six-month period (Pugh et al., 2021). Key ML concepts applied: Supervised learning, Classification, Feature engineering

Finance—Fraud Detection: A major credit card company developed an anomaly detection system to identify fraudulent transactions in real time. The system employed a combination of supervised and unsupervised learning techniques. Supervised models were trained on historical fraud data, while unsupervised clustering algorithms detected unusual patterns that might indicate new fraud tactics. This hybrid approach increased fraud detection rates by 37% while reducing false positives by 22%, saving the company millions in potential losses (Ogunlami, 2023). Key ML concepts applied: Supervised and unsupervised learning, Anomaly detection, Real-time processing.

E-commerce: Recommendation Systems. An online retailer implemented a collaborative filtering system to provide personalized product recommendations. The system analyzed user behavior, purchase history, and product characteristics using matrix factorization techniques. This approach increased click-through rates on recommended products by 45% and boosted overall sales by 12% within the first quarter of implementation. Key ML concepts applied: Unsupervised learning, Collaborative filtering, Feature engineering.

Manufacturing—Predictive Maintenance: A large automotive manufacturer employed ML to predict equipment failures before they occur. Using sensor data from machinery, they developed a model that combined regression techniques for predicting time-to-failure and classification for identifying the type of potential failure. This system reduced unplanned downtime by 35% and maintenance costs by 20%, significantly improving operational efficiency (Oza, 2024). Key ML concepts applied: Regression, Classification, Time series analysis.

Environmental Science—Climate Prediction: Climate scientists use ML models to improve long-term climate predictions. Simply by applying deep learning techniques to historical climate data and satellite imagery, they created models that could more accurately predict extreme weather events. These models demonstrated a 30% improvement in predicting the intensity and path of hurricanes compared to traditional methods, providing valuable lead time for disaster preparation (Tripathy et al., 2024). Key ML concepts applied: Deep learning, Time series forecasting, Computer vision.

Quizzes and Exercises

Quiz

1. What are the key differences between supervised and unsupervised learning? Provide an example of each.

2. Explain the concept of semi-supervised learning and how it differs from both supervised and unsupervised learning.

3. What is reinforcement learning, and in what types of problems is it commonly used?

4. Describe the difference between classification and regression problems. Provide an example of each.

5. What is the main goal of clustering algorithms? Name two common clustering techniques.

Exercises

1. **Supervised Learning Classification Exercise:** Using a publicly available dataset (such as the Iris dataset or the Titanic dataset), implement a simple classification algorithm (such as logistic regression or a decision tree). Train the model, make predictions, and calculate accuracy, precision, and recall. Discuss the results and any insights gained from the exercise.

2. **Unsupervised Learning Clustering Exercise:** Using a dataset of your choice (such as customer segmentation data), implement the K-means clustering algorithm. Experiment with different numbers of clusters and discuss how you would determine the optimal number of clusters. Visualize the results if possible.

3. **Feature Engineering Challenge:** Given a dataset with raw text data (like product reviews), propose and implement at least three feature engineering techniques to prepare the data for a sentiment analysis task. Explain your choices and how each technique might impact the model's performance.

Key Insights and Practical Takeaways

- **Learning Paradigms:** Understand the distinctions between supervised, unsupervised, semi-supervised, and reinforcement learning. Each paradigm serves different purposes and is suited for specific types of problems and data availability.

- **Supervised Learning:** Using labeled datasets for tasks like classification and regression. This approach is ideal for problems where you have clear input-output pairs, such as spam detection or sentiment analysis.

- **Unsupervised Learning:** Leverage this paradigm when working with unlabeled data to uncover hidden patterns or structures. It's particularly useful for tasks like customer segmentation or anomaly detection.

- **Algorithm Selection:** Choose algorithms based on your specific problem type. For instance, use classification algorithms for categorizing data, regression for predicting continuous values, and clustering for grouping similar data points.

- **Feature Engineering:** Invest time in creating and selecting relevant features. This process can significantly improve model performance by transforming raw data into more informative attributes.

- **Dimensionality Reduction:** Apply techniques like PCA or t-SNE to manage high-dimensional data, improving model efficiency and mitigating the curse of dimensionality.

- **Hybrid Approaches:** Don't hesitate to combine different learning paradigms or algorithms when tackling complex problems. For instance, using both supervised and unsupervised techniques in fraud detection systems.

CHAPTER 3

Fundamental System Design Principles

Designing scalable and efficient ML systems involves understanding the fundamental system design principles that form the backbone of any robust application. These principles guide the creation of systems capable of managing increased user loads as well as ensuring their continued reliability and ease of maintenance. As you go deeper into this chapter, you'll find out how these foundational concepts are important for building systems that perform consistently well under varying conditions. The ability to anticipate growth and maintain integrity while adapting to ever-evolving technological demands is what sets successful ML initiatives apart.

Throughout this chapter, we will explore the main pillars of scalability, reliability, and maintainability, each critical in its own right for constructing formidable ML ecosystems. We'll unpack the strategies behind scaling infrastructures to accommodate surges in demand, ensuring that your applications remain responsive and effective as they grow. The discussion will then shift towards maintaining system reliability, highlighting techniques and practices that prevent data loss or downtime, particularly in real-time scenarios. Finally, we'll look at how designing for maintainability allows for seamless updates and feature integration, supporting the agile adaptation needed in today's fast-paced tech landscape. Once you reach the end of this chapter, you'll have a great understanding of how to implement these principles effectively, preparing you for both practical challenges and interview scenarios in the world of ML.

Scalability, Reliability, and Maintainability

Scalability is about creating ML systems that handle increased loads without losing performance. Just like if an application suddenly gained popularity and needed to manage thousands of additional users overnight. A well-designed, scalable system absorbs this spike in usage seamlessly, rather than crumbling under pressure. Consider cloud-based solutions like Amazon Web Services (AWS) for their elasticity—where resources can be automatically added during peak times and released when demand decreases. This approach is cost-effective and crucial for future-proofing systems against growth.

Defining Scalability in the Context of ML Systems

When discussing scalability, it's essential to consider both horizontal and vertical scaling. Horizontal scaling is about adding more machines to handle the load, while vertical scaling refers to boosting the power of existing machines. Each has its pros and cons; horizontal scaling often provides greater flexibility and fault tolerance, as the workload can be spread across multiple nodes. Vertical scaling can be simpler to implement but tends to hit limits quickly. Deciding which path to take often depends on specific use cases and budget considerations.

Reliability of ML Pipelines

The reliability of ML pipelines is non-negotiable, especially when systems operate in real-time environments where downtime equates to lost data or revenue. Implementing robust error-handling mechanisms allows these systems to remain consistent even when unexpected issues arise. For instance, using techniques like transaction logging or checkpointing can help maintain integrity by recording operations so processes can resume from the last stable state after a failure.

Strategies for Building Reliable ML Pipelines

For ensuring reliability, employing failover strategies is vital. These strategies are all about redirecting workloads to backup systems when primary systems fail. In terms of application, think of critical services such as online banking—where any disruption could have severe consequences. Here, redundancy plays a key role, with everything from data sources to APIs being duplicated to provide backup options instantly should anything go awry.

Leveraging Containerization: A practical guideline for building reliable pipelines includes leveraging containerization through tools like Docker. Containers encapsulate code and dependencies, allowing applications to run consistently across various computing environments. This additional layer of abstraction facilitates testing and deployment as well as enhancing system resilience by isolating failures to individual containers.

Maintainability: This focuses on constructing modular and well-documented codebases that simplify updates and feature integration. In the fast-paced world of technology, software must evolve rapidly to meet user needs and incorporate cutting-edge algorithms. A modular design breaks down complex systems into manageable pieces, each responsible for a distinct function, making it easier to locate and fix bugs or improve performance.

Consider microservices architecture as a practical example of maintainability. They allow developers to build features independently, promoting quicker deployments and minimizing disruptions to current functionalities. When implemented correctly, this structure can dramatically reduce the time needed to bring new features to market—a significant advantage in competitive industries.

Documentation: This is another pillar of maintainability that shouldn't be overlooked. Clear, concise documentation is important and serves as a blueprint for both current team members and future developers. It acts as a map for exploring the complexities of the codebase, helping in quicker onboarding and knowledge transfer. Tools like Javadoc or Sphinx can automate parts of this process, generating documentation directly from code comments, and so, making sure accuracy and ease of use.

Version Control Systems: Another best practice is adopting version control systems like Git. Version control permits tracking of changes over time, allowing developers to revert to earlier states if new implementations introduce errors. Such systems also enhance collaboration by allowing team members to work concurrently and merge their contributions efficiently.

While embracing scalability, reliability, and maintainability individually increases an ML system's robustness, it's also important to recognize the interplay between these principles. For instance, enhancing scalability through additional servers might complicate maintenance efforts if not managed properly. Similarly, a highly reliable system that lacks scalability may struggle under growing demand.

Data Storage and Processing

When building ML systems, effective data management is just as vital. The choices you make about how and where to store your data can significantly impact the performance and scalability of your applications. One of the fundamental decisions is between using relational or NoSQL databases. Relational databases, like MySQL and PostgreSQL, are structured and use tables to organize data, making them ideal for applications that require complex queries and strong consistency. They excel in transactional environments where ACID (Atomicity, Consistency, Isolation, Durability) properties are essential. However, their rigid schema can become a bottleneck when dealing with unstructured data or rapidly changing data models.

On the other hand, NoSQL databases such as MongoDB and Cassandra offer flexibility through their schema-less design, which can handle unstructured data more efficiently. These databases are often used in scenarios where scalability and high throughput are more critical than strict consistency, making them suitable for handling large volumes of data with variable schemas. To give you an example, if you're working on a recommendation system that needs to process and analyze user-generated content in real time, NoSQL might be the way to go. As a guideline, if your main concern is horizontal scaling and handling large data sets quickly, consider leaning towards NoSQL solutions. But if your focus is on maintaining consistency and relational integrity, a traditional relational database might serve you better.

Distributed Storage Systems for Large-Scale ML Applications

Beyond choosing the right type of database, the method of storing and accessing your data at scale is another vital consideration. Distributed storage systems like Hadoop and HDFS were designed to handle massive amounts of data efficiently. These systems break data into chunks stored across multiple nodes, allowing for fault tolerance and parallel processing. This setup can really improve the speed and reliability of data access in ML applications that require processing large datasets. For example, an image recognition system trained on billions of images would benefit from Hadoop's ability to partition and manage data across clusters, providing both resilience and performance enhancements.

Data Processing Frameworks for Batch- and Stream-Processing

Once your data is effectively stored, how you process it becomes relevant. Data processing frameworks such as Apache Spark and Flink come into play by offering robust solutions for both batch and stream-processing. Apache Spark, known for its in-memory data processing capabilities, is excellent for iterative algorithms and interactive data analysis. It's designed to handle large-scale data processing tasks and can run seamlessly alongside Hadoop HDFS. On the flip side, Apache Flink is renowned for its low-latency stream-processing, making it perfect for real-time analytics and event-driven applications.

For example, if you're developing a fraud detection system that needs to analyze transactions in real-time to prevent suspicious activities, using Flink could significantly enhance your system's capabilities. Both Spark and Flink provide APIs for Java, Scala, and Python, making them accessible to developers familiar with these languages. A general guideline here is to choose a framework based on your latency requirements—Spark for batch-processing and iterative tasks, while Flink suits near-instantaneous, streaming operations.

Optimizing Data Access Patterns for ML Workloads

Optimizing data access patterns is also essential to allow quick retrieval and manipulation of data. This involves techniques like indexing and caching, which can dramatically reduce latency and boost throughput for your ML workloads. When creating indexes on frequently queried attributes, you can retrieve data faster than scanning entire datasets. Similarly, using caching mechanisms like Redis or Memcached allows you to store frequently accessed data in memory temporarily, reducing the load on your primary database and speeding up access times.

In practice, suppose you have a recommendation engine that updates user preferences based on recent activity. Caching these preferences can enhance the system's responsiveness, providing users with instant recommendations without querying the database repeatedly. Indexing your datasets appropriately, making sure that even as they grow, your system remains agile and responsive. The guideline here is straightforward: if your application involves repetitive data access patterns or requires fast response times, investing in comprehensive indexing and caching strategies is well worth the effort.

Quizzes and Exercises

Quiz

1. What does scalability mean in the context of ML systems? How does it differ from traditional software system scalability?

2. Name three strategies for improving the reliability of ML pipelines.

3. What are the key trade-offs to consider when balancing scalability, reliability, and system complexity in ML system design?

4. Compare and contrast relational and NoSQL databases in the context of ML applications. When would you choose one over the other?

5. Explain the concept of distributed storage systems and why they are important for large-scale ML applications.

Exercises

- **Scalability Design Exercise:** Design a high-level architecture for a scalable image classification system that can handle millions of image uploads per day. Consider aspects such as data storage, processing pipelines, and model serving. Explain how your design addresses potential scaling challenges.

- **Reliability Analysis:** Analyze a real-world ML system failure. Identify the potential causes of the failure and propose three specific measures that could have been implemented to prevent or mitigate the issue. Explain the rationale behind each measure.

- **Database Selection Scenario:** You're designing an ML system for a social media platform that needs to store user profiles, posts, and interaction data, as well as trained ML models. Propose a database solution (or combination of solutions) for this scenario. Justify your choice(s) and explain how it addresses the specific needs of the platform and its ML components.

Key Insights and Practical Takeaways

- **Scalability:** Design systems that can handle increased loads without performance degradation. Consider both horizontal scaling (adding more machines) and vertical scaling (boosting existing machine power) based on your specific use case and budget.

- **Reliability:** Implement robust error-handling mechanisms and failover strategies to ensure consistent operation, especially in real-time environments. Use techniques like transaction logging and checkpointing to maintain system integrity during failures.

- **Maintainability:** Construct modular and well-documented codebases to simplify updates and feature integration. Adopt microservices architecture for independent feature development and quicker deployments.

- **Containerization:** Leverage tools like Docker to encapsulate code and dependencies, enhancing system resilience and facilitating consistent deployment across various environments.

- **Version Control:** Implement version control systems like Git to track changes, enable collaboration, and allow for easy rollbacks if needed.

- **Database Selection:** Choose between relational (e.g., MySQL, PostgreSQL) and NoSQL (e.g., MongoDB, Cassandra) databases based on your data structure and consistency requirements. Use relational databases for complex queries and strong consistency, and NoSQL for flexibility and high throughput.

- **Distributed Storage:** Utilize distributed storage systems like Hadoop and HDFS to handle massive datasets efficiently, enabling fault tolerance and parallel processing.

- **Data Processing Frameworks:** Employ frameworks like Apache Spark for batch-processing and iterative algorithms, and Apache Flink for low-latency stream-processing and real-time analytics.

CHAPTER 4

Machine Learning Lifecycle

The ML lifecycle is an intriguing path that encompasses a series of essential stages, each as important as the next. It all begins with understanding the lifeblood of models: data. Without quality data collection and thoughtful feature engineering, even the most robust algorithms may fail to deliver. This initiation into ML sets the stage for various considerations and strategies essential for bringing models to life. As the cycle progresses, it's more than just about deploying a model; it's about crafting it meticulously from ground zero, knowing that every piece fits perfectly within the grander puzzle. This exploration reveals how different elements come together and why each step, from data preparation to model reality checks, becomes a story in itself.

Here, we will focus on the nuances of what makes a successful ML project tick from start to finish. With a focus on data collection techniques, you'll find out how choosing relevant datasets impacts model performance right out of the gate. The art of preprocessing and feature engineering will be talked about, showing you how raw data transforms into insightful, actionable intelligence. You'll know how model selection processes intertwine with the specific needs of your project, learning about training intricacies and hyperparameter tuning along the way. Finally, venturing into deployment and monitoring, the chapter uncovers strategies to integrate models seamlessly into production environments while ensuring their continual effectiveness through vigilant oversight and adaptation. Once you reach the end of the chapter, you will have a comprehensive understanding of what it takes to bring a ML model from conception to operational success.

Data Collection, Preprocessing, and Feature Engineering

In ML, data is the cornerstone that drives models to perform their tasks effectively. Making sure that there's high-quality inputs from the start can make the difference between a well-functioning system and one that fails to meet expectations. Let's get into the foundational stages of data handling, starting with strategies for efficient data collection and labeling.

Strategies for Efficient Data Collection and Labeling

Comprehensive and relevant data collection is integral to model success. Strategies for data collection should not just aim at amassing large datasets but focus on relevance and accuracy. Consider domain-specific details that might influence the data's applicability to your model's goal. Say that you're working on a natural language processing task in healthcare; gathering health-related text from diverse, reliable sources can enrich your dataset. Surveys and direct user feedback are methods that may add human insights into data gathering, although they require meticulous planning to avoid biases.

To make sure the labels within this data are accurate, employing a precise labeling strategy is quite vital. Human annotation remains important, of course, especially when labeled data is scarce or complex. However, it's essential to train annotators thoroughly and double-check their work using inter-annotator agreement measures. The use of automated tools like NLP taggers or image labeling software can accelerate the process, though regular audits are necessary to verify accuracy.

Data Cleaning and Quality Assurance Techniques

Once you have your collected data, it's time to refine it through data cleaning and quality assurance. This step addresses the imperfections inherent in raw data, which often include duplicates, incoherent formats, and inconsistent units. Data cleaning tools, like OpenRefine or Python libraries, such as Pandas, help streamline this process by providing functionalities to handle these issues systematically.

Quality assurance goes hand-in-hand with data cleaning, focusing on dataset integrity and consistency. It's not uncommon for datasets to contain errors due to manual entry flaws or outdated sources. Verification processes are designed to catch these discrepancies. In practice, this might involve cross-referencing information against trusted databases or using statistical tests to detect anomalies.

Handling Missing Data and Outliers

Handling missing data and outliers is another significant aspect of data preparation. Missing values could arise from various reasons, including nonresponse or equipment failure during measurements. Addressing them is crucial, as they can skew model interpretation. Imputation methods such as mean substitution or regression imputation help fill gaps without substantial losses in data utility. Meanwhile, excluding entire records is an option, though it must be done cautiously to avoid reducing dataset diversity.

Outliers, on the other hand, might play a deceptive role. They can hint at genuine, rare phenomena or merely result from errors. Techniques like z-score or IQR (Interquartile Range) analysis are beneficial in identifying outliers. Once identified, outliers can be repositioned, capped, or omitted based on the context and their potential impact on the model.

Feature Engineering

Turning raw data into informative features through feature engineering is perhaps the most creative phase of data handling. Carefully crafted features lead to more insightful models. Feature engineering involves transforming raw attributes into structured formats and refining them to encapsulate deeper meanings. For example, categorical variables like "city" might be converted into dummy variables, allowing models to understand each city's unique contribution separately. Text data, which is abundant in modern applications, can be converted into numerical entities using techniques like TF-IDF (Term Frequency-Inverse Document Frequency) or word embeddings, thereby capturing semantic richness.

Also, considering temporal aspects and geographical traits during feature creation can uncover patterns that are not immediately obvious in raw data. Time-series data might benefit from lag features, offering your model historical context, which can dramatically improve forecasting accuracy.

Before finalizing your dataset, ensure that all features align with the model objectives. Irrelevant features may introduce noise, leading models astray. A preliminary correlation analysis can highlight these unnecessary features, guiding you toward a cleaner, more effective feature set.

Model Selection, Training, Deployment, and Monitoring

In the ML lifecycle, efficiently selecting, training, deploying, and maintaining models is one of the most important things when it comes to achieving optimal performance and reliability. The first step in this journey has to do with wisely choosing the right algorithms based on both the specific problem at hand and the characteristics of the dataset. Not all algorithms fit all scenarios; understanding the nuances of each algorithm can significantly impact model success. For example, decision trees might be suitable for their interpretability, while neural networks excel with large datasets where deep patterns need recognition. Grasping these distinctions helps in aligning your choice with the problem requirements, leading to better performance outcomes.

Hyperparameter Tuning Techniques

Once an appropriate algorithm is chosen, the next focus should be refining the model through hyperparameter tuning. Techniques like grid search, random search, and Bayesian optimization are invaluable here. Grid search exhaustively searches through a set of manually specified hyperparameters, offering thoroughness but often at a high computational cost. Random search, however, selects random combinations and tends to be more efficient. Bayesian optimization takes it a step further by using past evaluation results to choose the next set of parameters, often speeding up the convergence process toward the best parameters. These methods collectively provide avenues to enhance the model's accuracy, balancing between exploration and exploitation of hyperparameter spaces.

Model Deployment Strategies

The transition from training to deployment introduces unique challenges. Using strategic deployment methodologies such as canary releases and blue-green deployments allows seamless integration into production environments with minimal risk. Canary releases involve gradually exposing a change to a small set of users before a full-scale release, helping to catch unforeseen issues early. Blue-green deployments maintain two parallel environments—one active (blue) and one idle (green). This method permits easy rollback if necessary and ensures continuous service availability. Such strategies are essential not only for reducing downtime but also for minimizing disruptions and ensuring that any updates are smoothly transitioned into live settings.

Monitoring Deployment Strategies

Monitoring deployed models in production is a dynamic aspect of sustaining a reliable ML system. Performance monitoring allows the model to continue to deliver expected outcomes, which could otherwise degrade over time due to external changes—a phenomenon known as data drift. Unnoticed, data drift can lead to significant declines in model effectiveness. Implementing robust feedback loops is relevant for maintaining model health. Such loops involve regularly feeding new data back into the training processes and adjusting models according to real-time insights. A well-established feedback mechanism assists in timely retraining and updating of models, preserving their alignment with user expectations and evolving data landscapes.

Regularly analyzing feedback data helps identify patterns or trends that might warrant attention or adjustments. Should there be a consistent shift in input data patterns, it signifies that the model assumptions may no longer hold true, needing retraining with updated data. Automation can play avital role in this process, triggering alerts and initiating retraining protocols without manual intervention, thus boosting efficiency and response times.

Keeping It Transparent

Finally, maintaining transparency throughout these processes remains relevant for stakeholder confidence and regulatory compliance. Documenting performance metrics and modifications made during retraining empowers teams to track model evolution effectively. Furthermore, clear communication of model changes to users solidifies trust and fosters an understanding of the benefits provided by the updates.

Quizzes and Exercises

Quiz

1. What are three key strategies for efficient data collection and labeling in ML projects?

2. Describe two techniques for handling missing data in a dataset. What are the pros and cons of each?

3. What is data augmentation, and how can it improve model performance?

4. Explain the difference between feature selection and feature engineering. Provide an example of each.

5. How do you handle categorical variables in feature engineering? Name two common techniques.

Exercises

1. **Data Cleaning and Preprocessing:** Given a dataset with missing values, outliers, and inconsistent formatting, outline a step-by-step process for cleaning and preprocessing the data. Implement your process using a programming language of your choice and explain the rationale behind each step.

2. **Feature Engineering Challenge:** For a text classification problem (such as sentiment analysis of product reviews), propose and implement at least three feature engineering techniques. Explain how each technique might impact the model's performance and any potential drawbacks.

3. **Model Selection and Hyperparameter Tuning:** Choose a publicly available dataset and a ML task. Implement at least two different algorithms for this task and use both grid search and random search for hyperparameter tuning. Compare the results and discuss the trade-offs between the methods.

As we finish this chapter and with it, the exploration of the ML model development pipeline, it's quite clear how each stage intricately ties into the next, creating a cohesive framework. From gathering and refining data to sculpting it into meaningful features, every step builds on itself to form a solid foundation for subsequent processes.

Key Insights and Practical Takeaways

- **Data Preparation:** Ensure thorough data preprocessing, cleaning, and feature engineering to set a solid foundation for your model's success.

- **Hyperparameter Tuning:** Invest time in meticulous hyperparameter tuning to push your model's performance to its optimal level. Use techniques like random search or Bayesian optimization to enhance efficiency.

- **Deployment Strategies:** Implement robust deployment methods like canary releases and blue-green deployments to integrate models smoothly and minimize production risks.

- **Monitoring and Maintenance:** Regularly monitor your deployed models to catch performance degradation due to data drift. Establish feedback loops to trigger retraining automatically and keep your model aligned with evolving data patterns.

CHAPTER 5

Basic ML System Architectures

Building basic ML system architectures is a journey into the heart of how modern data-driven decisions are made. The main pillars of these architectures have to do with an interplay between batch-processing and real-time prediction systems, each serving distinct yet complementary roles in the landscape of ML. Visualize batch-processing as a diligent worker who collects vast amounts of data over time, meticulously analyzing it to uncover patterns and trends that can influence strategic decisions. This process may not be immediate, but it's thorough, providing a great understanding of the data at hand. Meanwhile, picture real-time prediction systems are nimble sprinters designed to act on data instantly. They thrive on the urgency of what's happening now, delivering quick insights that can make or break competitive advantage in fast-paced environments such as financial markets or customer interactions.

In this chapter, we'll look deeper into the components and workflows that form the backbone of these essential systems. For those transitioning into ML roles, understanding these architectures is key to designing effective solutions tailored to specific needs. From exploring how data moves through batch pipelines fueled by tools like Apache Hadoop and Spark to unraveling the microservices infrastructure that supports swift real-time predictions, you will gain practical insight into what makes these systems tick. We'll also touch upon the critical balance between latency and accuracy, a challenge ever-present when crafting models for immediate decision-making. It doesn't matter if you're prepping for interviews, seeking to solidify your knowledge base, or simply expanding your understanding of industry-standard practices; this chapter will offer a foundational lens through which to view system design in ML.

Batch-Processing and Real-Time Prediction Systems

Within ML, understanding the architecture of batch-processing and real-time prediction systems is a very important part of it. These systems are the foundation of how data is processed and interpreted to make impactful decisions.

Components of a Batch-Processing ML System

Batch-processing systems are relevant in managing large-scale datasets. In simple words, these systems consist of several key components: data collection, storage, computation, and output generation. Data is often collected from various sources and stored in databases or warehouses. Once there is enough accumulated data, batch processes are executed at scheduled intervals. This is where computation takes place, turning raw data into meaningful insights through algorithms or models that analyze patterns, trends, or anomalies. The results are then generated as outputs, ready for further analysis or decision-making.

Advantages and Limitations of Batch-Processing

However, batch-processing isn't without its drawbacks. While efficient at handling extensive volumes of data, you must acknowledge its primary limitation—latency. Since data is processed in batches and not in real-time, any decisions based on this data can be delayed, which might not be ideal in scenarios requiring immediate insight. For example, consider an e-commerce platform analyzing customer purchase trends. While batch-processing can give a comprehensive view of buying patterns over time, it may not promptly signal a sudden change in purchasing behavior due to a flash sale.

Despite these limitations, batch-processing remains indispensable, particularly when dealing with massive datasets requiring periodic updates. Its efficiency and scalability make it a go-to option for many large-scale operations.

Tools and Frameworks for Implementing Batch ML Pipelines

The implementation of batch ML pipelines is significantly optimized by tools like Apache Hadoop and Apache Spark. These frameworks have become integral in constructing effective batch-processing systems. Apache Hadoop offers a distributed computing model, allowing data to be processed across clusters of computers, and so, enhancing scalability and fault tolerance. Meanwhile, Apache Spark offers faster computation by leveraging in-memory processing, making it highly suitable for iterative ML tasks. When combined, these tools empower developers to build good batch pipelines that are equipped for complex computations, giving them the flexibility to handle varying workload demands effectively.

Use Cases and Examples of Batch-Processing in ML

Real-time prediction systems, on the other hand, cater to scenarios where latency is a critical factor. Unlike batch systems, these architectures are designed to provide low-latency inference, meaning they can quickly analyze incoming data and generate predictions almost instantaneously. This capability positions them as ideal solutions for applications such as fraud detection, financial trading, or personalized marketing, where timely decision-making can significantly impact outcomes.

To achieve rapid decision-making, real-time systems often employ microservice architectures. Microservices break down applications into smaller, independent services that communicate with each other. Each service handles specific functions, enabling the overall system to process requests efficiently and adapt to changes swiftly. This modular approach allows for the prediction system to remain agile and scalable, capable of expanding as application demands grow.

Designing real-time systems involves addressing challenges like balancing speed with accuracy. Low-latency predictions require optimized models that can rapidly process and infer data without compromising on the precision of the output. This often needs a trade-off, and engineers must carefully design systems to meet the unique requirements of each use case.

In practice, companies leverage both batch and real-time systems depending on their needs. For instance, a streaming service might use batch-processing to analyze user engagement over weeks or months, helping them refine content strategies. Simultaneously, they may deploy real-time systems to recommend content during a user's session based on current viewing behaviors, making sure that there's relevance as well as improving the user experience.

Recommendation Systems

Recommendation systems are essential components in today's digital landscape, guiding users through an overwhelming array of options by suggesting relevant products, services, or content. These systems rely on several main architectural elements designed to customize suggestions effectively. Among these fundamental components are filtering mechanisms, user profiles, and item databases.

Core Components of Recommendation System Architecture

Filtering mechanisms play an important role in narrowing down the vast pool of options available to a user. They serve as the foundation of recommendation systems, sifting through enormous datasets to identify items that align with user preferences. Each user's profile is crafted through a combination of explicit data, such as past purchases or ratings, and implicit behavior, like browsing history and click patterns. Together, these elements create a detailed picture of the user's interests, allowing for precise recommendations.

Similarly, item databases form another vital part of the recommendation architecture. These databases house the extensive inventory of items, including their attributes, availability, and any associated metadata—a critical resource used by filtering algorithms to match items with user preferences efficiently.

Collaborative Filtering vs. Content-Based Filtering Approaches

When it comes to methodologies within recommendation systems, collaborative filtering, and content-based filtering stand out. Collaborative filtering operates on the assumption that users who agreed in the past will continue to agree in the future. It leverages patterns in collective user behaviors to generate recommendations. For example, if two users have similar tastes, the system might suggest books read by one user to the other. This technique can be further divided into user-based and item-based methods. The user-based approach looks for similarities between users' behavior, while the item-based method examines the relationships between different items based on user interactions.

On the flip side, content-based filtering bypasses the need for extensive user base information. Instead, it focuses on the attributes of items themselves. When analyzing item features—such as keywords, descriptions, or genres—it's important to align them with the user's known preferences. If a user often reads mystery novels, a content-based recommender would suggest new releases from the same genre, relying heavily on item characteristics rather than user behavior patterns.

Handling Cold Start Problems in Recommendation Systems

Despite their effectiveness, both methods encounter specific challenges. One notable issue is the cold start problem, which arises when there is insufficient data about new users or items. In these scenarios, traditional filtering approaches struggle to provide accurate recommendations. This is where hybrid models come into play, combining elements of both collaborative and content-based filtering to offer a more balanced solution. If integrating user preference data with item attributes, hybrid models can jump-start the recommendation process, offering relevant suggestions even when data is scarce.

The implementation of hybrid models addresses the cold start problem and enhances personalization by leveraging a wider array of data points. For example, Netflix employs a hybrid approach to recommend movies and shows. It doesn't solely depend on what similar viewers watched (collaborative filtering) but also considers movie genres and actors liked by the user (content-based filtering).

Scalability Challenges and Solutions in Large-Scale Recommenders

Scalability is another significant challenge for large-scale recommendation systems, especially as they grow to accommodate an ever-increasing user base and expanding item catalog. As these systems scale, maintaining performance becomes crucial to delivering timely and relevant recommendations. Solutions like parallel computing and horizontal scaling are instrumental in tackling these scaling issues.

Parallel computing: This allows the distribution of computational tasks across multiple processors, thereby speeding up the processing time. This efficiency is particularly beneficial for handling large datasets and complex algorithms common in recommendation systems. Say that a company like Amazon uses parallel processing to manage its recommendation engine, allowing fast and reliable service despite its massive catalog and user count.

Horizontal scaling: On the other hand, this technique involves adding more machines or servers to distribute the workload, preventing bottlenecks and enhancing system reliability. Unlike vertical scaling, which enhances a single server's capacity, horizontal scaling offers flexibility and redundancy, vital for uninterrupted service during peak usage times.

Quizzes and Exercises

Quiz

1. What are the main components of a batch-processing ML system? How do they interact with each other?

2. Name three advantages and two limitations of batch-processing in ML systems.

3. What is the key difference between batch-processing and real-time prediction systems in terms of data handling?

4. Describe two strategies for optimizing low-latency ML inference in real-time prediction systems.

5. What is the purpose of caching in real-time ML systems, and how does it improve performance?

Exercises

1. **Batch-Processing System Design:** Design a batch-processing ML system for analyzing customer churn in a telecommunications company. Include components for data ingestion, preprocessing, model training, and result storage. Explain how each component interacts and propose suitable tools or frameworks for implementation.

2. **Real-time Prediction System Optimization:** You're tasked with optimizing a real-time prediction system for a high-traffic e-commerce website. The system currently struggles with high latency during peak hours. Propose three specific optimizations to improve the system's performance, explaining the rationale and expected impact of each.

3. **Recommendation System Architecture:** Sketch the architecture for a hybrid recommendation system that combines collaborative and content-based filtering. Explain how the system would handle: (a) New users (cold start problem); (b) Real-time updates based on user interactions; (c) Scaling to millions of users and items.

Key Insights and Practical Takeaways

- **Batch-Processing Systems:** Understand the components of batch-processing systems, including data collection, storage, computation, and output generation. These systems are ideal for handling large-scale datasets and periodic analysis.

- **Real-time Prediction Systems:** Recognize the importance of low-latency inference in scenarios requiring immediate insights. Implement microservices architectures to enable quick analysis of incoming data and rapid decision-making.

- **Balancing Latency and Accuracy:** When designing real-time systems, carefully balance the trade-off between speed and accuracy. Optimize models to process data quickly without compromising on the precision of outputs.

- **Recommendation System Architecture:** Implement core components such as filtering mechanisms, user profiles, and item databases to create effective recommendation systems.

- **Filtering Techniques:** Understand the differences between collaborative filtering and content-based filtering. Use collaborative filtering when leveraging user behavior patterns and content-based filtering when focusing on item attributes.

- **Scalability Solutions:** Employ techniques like parallel computing and horizontal scaling to manage large-scale recommendation systems. These approaches help maintain performance as user bases and item catalogs grow.

- **Cold Start Problem:** Address the cold start problem in recommendation systems by using hybrid models that can provide relevant suggestions even when user or item data is limited.

- **Tools and Frameworks:** Utilize tools like Apache Hadoop and Apache Spark for implementing efficient batch ML pipelines. These frameworks enhance scalability and computation speed for large-scale data processing.

CHAPTER 6

Data Management for ML Systems

Data management for ML systems is an important component in bridging the gap between theoretical models and practical applications. The intricacies of how data is stored, processed, and accessed play a role in influencing the performance and efficiency of ML endeavors. In this chapter, we'll be talking about the multifaceted terrain of data storage solutions, exploring the differences between SQL and NoSQL databases, each with its own set of advantages and disadvantages. Understanding these distinctions helps tailor data architecture to specific ML scenarios. Whether it's dealing with structured rows and columns or managing a more free-form collection of diverse data types, choosing the right database can set the foundation for seamless data handling.

As we talk a little more about it, the focus will shift to the fascinating world of data pipelines and ETL processes, essential for feeding ML systems with clean, organized, and reliable data. From extraction to transformation and finally loading, each stage of the pipeline demands meticulous attention to allow data quality and relevance. We'll unpack various tools and strategies that facilitate these processes, such as scheduling complex workflows and implementing real-time data streaming. Alongside these technical insights, we'll also look at the best practices for scaling systems to accommodate growing datasets and maintaining vibrant and efficient ML operations.

Data Storage Solutions (SQL vs. NoSQL)

When selecting a database system for ML applications, it's important to understand the distinctions between relational and non-relational databases. Each type of database has its own strengths and weaknesses, particularly in handling structured versus unstructured data necessary for ML.

Comparing Relational and Non-Relational Databases for ML Applications

Relational databases, such as MySQL and PostgreSQL, excel at managing structured data. They organize information into tables with predefined schemas, which makes them ideal for datasets where relationships between different types of data are well-defined. If you're working with tabular data from business processes, relational databases can effectively handle complex queries and transactions. On the downside, they may not be as flexible when dealing with rapidly changing or varied data types typical in many ML scenarios.

On the other hand, non-relational databases, often referred to as NoSQL databases, are designed for diverse data models and are adept at handling unstructured data. Popular NoSQL databases like MongoDB and Cassandra allow for greater flexibility by supporting document-oriented, key-value, wide-column, and graph formats. This adaptability is beneficial when you're dealing with large volumes of data that don't fit neatly into a tabular format, such as social media content or IoT sensor data. However, this freedom comes at the cost of some features offered by relational systems, like ACID transactions, although newer NoSQL solutions are beginning to address these limitations.

Choosing the Right Database Based on Data Structure and Access Patterns

Once you know whether your data is more structured or unstructured, assessing the compatibility of various databases with different ML use cases becomes vital. This is about examining the specific intricacies of your data structure and the access patterns you expect. For example, consider a scenario where real-time data processing is relevant, such as in recommendation systems. Here, a database that supports fast read and write operations and can handle high throughput rates might be necessary. DynamoDB and Redis are examples that are used for such needs.

When evaluating databases, it's also essential to consider the nature of the access patterns. Databases like Elasticsearch are designed for full-text search capabilities, making them suitable for applications requiring robust search functions, such as customer service analytics that sift through large amounts of textual data. Meanwhile, graph databases like Neo4j excel in applications that require understanding complex relationships, such as fraud detection or social network analysis.

Something to think about when it comes to choosing the right database is to conduct a thorough analysis of your ML model's requirements. Ask yourself questions like, *What kind of queries will be run frequently? Will the database need to support transactions, or is eventual consistency acceptable? How scalable does the solution need to be to accommodate future data growth?*

Scaling Database Systems for Large ML Datasets

Speaking of scalability, efficiently scaling database systems as the volume and velocity of ML datasets increase is another critical consideration. As datasets grow, so do the demands on storage and computational resources. Techniques such as sharding, replication, and load balancing become very important. Sharding is about dividing a database into smaller, manageable pieces that can be distributed across multiple servers. This distribution helps maintain performance levels as data grows. Replication, on the other hand, involves copying data across multiple nodes to ensure reliability and availability, even if one node fails.

Cloud-based solutions like Amazon RDS or Google Cloud Spanner provide built-in scalability features, allowing you to focus more on developing ML models rather than managing infrastructure. These services automatically adjust resource allocation based on demand and offer a seamless way to handle fluctuating loads inherent to ML workflows.

Best Practices for Data Modeling in ML Contexts

With scaling strategies in place, attention should turn towards best practices for data modeling to optimize ML processes. Data modeling encompasses structuring data in a way that aligns with the objectives of the ML application while maximizing performance and efficiency. A well-thought-out data model ensures that ML algorithms have quick access to relevant data, reducing latency and improving outcomes.

For example, denormalization in databases—storing redundant copies of data to reduce the need for complex joins—can be effective in speeding up read-heavy workloads common in ML applications. Considering the right indexing strategy can significantly improve query performance. Choosing between primary and secondary indexes, and deciding how much memory to allocate to index storage, can have a significant impact on the speed and efficiency of data retrieval, directly influencing the training and prediction phases of ML models.

Lastly, always measure performance regularly. Using metrics and monitoring tools to continually assess how your database system handles the evolving demands of ML applications. Adjust your strategies and optimize configurations based on these insights to make sure that data management remains robust as you scale up efforts with larger datasets and more sophisticated models.

Data Pipelines and ETL Processes

Building efficient ETL (Extract, Transform, Load) pipelines are fundamental to managing data for ML systems. These pipelines play a role in allowing that data to be clean, well-structured, and ready for analysis. For ML use cases, designing these pipelines involves understanding specific data needs and patterns. A robust ETL pipeline should be customized to handle various stages of data processing seamlessly. For example, during extraction, it's important to pull data from multiple sources efficiently. This can include structured databases or real-time data streams. Leveraging connectors capable of accessing different data formats will enhance the ingestion process. Using APIs to fetch data directly from web services or integrating directly with data warehouses can streamline this stage significantly.

Transformation Phase

The transformation phase is where data gets cleaned and prepped. This step often involves deduplication, handling missing values, and normalizing data. For ML, it's critical to transform data into a format suitable for models, which might involve one-hot encoding categorical variables or scaling numerical attributes. Setting up transformation workflows that can be easily updated as data requirements evolve is just as important. Journaling transformations can help in maintaining consistency, making sure that once models are trained, new data arrivals go through identical preprocessing steps.

Once data is transformed, you should load it effectively into a target database or warehouse. This process must be optimized not only for accuracy but also for speed to accommodate large volumes typical in ML scenarios. Techniques like partitioning and indexing can help improve query performance when accessing this data later on.

Tools and Frameworks for Building Robust Data Pipelines

When constructing these pipelines, choosing the right tools makes a significant difference, for example:

Apache Airflow and Luigi: These are quite popular among engineers due to their ability to schedule and automate complex workflows. Luigi excels at handling intricate dependency management and providing visualizations of task execution.

Airflow: This provides an intuitive interface for managing task dependencies and scheduling jobs. Both Airflow and Luigi enable building scalable, repeatable workflows, which is essential for maintaining the integrity of ML applications over time. To decide between them, consider factors like your team's familiarity with Python (as both are Python-based) and the level of support required for parallel task execution.

Handling Data Quality and Consistency in ETL Processes

The importance of data quality has to be once again highlighted. Poor data quality and inconsistencies are the primary culprits of erroneous ML predictions. Strategies for addressing these issues focus on establishing rigorous validation checks at each ETL stage. Data validation rules should be implemented to catch anomalies or incorrect entries early. Automating these checks ensures continuous monitoring and immediate rectification of data discrepancies. Another effective strategy is data profiling, which helps catalog data elements to understand their structure and content better, leading to more informed decisions regarding cleaning and normalizing strategies.

Optimizing Pipelines for Performance and Reliability

Optimizing data pipelines is an ongoing practice aimed at achieving maximal performance and reliability.

Incrementally Load Data: This technique updates only changed records rather than reprocessing entire datasets. This approach reduces resource consumption and accelerates the data update process.

Parallel Processing: This method can also be employed to handle large datasets faster by dividing tasks across multiple processors or machines. Moreover, streaming data processes, using technologies like Apache Kafka, allows data to be ingested and processed in real-time, which is crucial for applications requiring immediate insights.

Automation: This is important in optimizing data pipelines. Automating mundane or repetitive tasks frees up developers to focus on more strategic activities while reducing the margin for error. Implementing automated alerts and notifications for failed tasks or unusual patterns allows quick responses to potential issues, minimizing downtime and data contamination risks. Additionally, pipelines can benefit from load-testing simulations prior to deployment, which helps predict behavior under varying conditions and identifies bottlenecks that could impede performance.

Maintaining documentation: You can do this throughout the ETL lifecycle, which is great for boosting pipeline efficacy. Well-documented steps and procedures facilitate easier troubleshooting, quicker onboarding of new team members, and more agile adaptation to future changes or enhancements in the data ecosystem.

Quizzes and Exercises

Quiz

1. What are the key differences between SQL and NoSQL databases in the context of ML applications?

2. Name three factors to consider when choosing between a relational and non-relational database for an ML system.

3. How does data modeling in ML contexts differ from traditional data modeling?

4. What is an ETL pipeline, and why is it important in ML systems?

5. Name two popular tools or frameworks for building data pipelines in ML systems.

Exercises

1. **Database Selection Case Study:** You're designing an ML system for a social media platform that needs to store user profiles, posts, interaction data, and trained ML models. Propose a database solution (or combination of solutions) for this scenario. Justify your choice(s) and explain how it addresses the specific needs of the platform and its ML components.

2. **ETL Pipeline Design:** Design an ETL pipeline for a sentiment analysis system that processes customer reviews from multiple e-commerce platforms. Include steps for data extraction, cleaning, transformation, and loading. Specify which tools or frameworks you would use at each stage and explain your choices.

3. **Data Modeling for ML:** Create a data model for a recommendation system that suggests movies to users. Include entities for users, movies, ratings, and any other relevant data. Explain how your model supports both the storage of raw data and the features used by the ML model.

Key Insights and Practical Takeaways

- **Database Selection:** Choose between SQL (relational) and NoSQL (non-relational) databases based on your data structure and access patterns. SQL databases are ideal for structured data with complex relationships, while NoSQL databases offer flexibility for unstructured or diverse data types.

- **Scalability Strategies:** Implement techniques like sharding, replication, and load balancing to efficiently scale database systems as ML datasets grow. Consider cloud-based solutions for built-in scalability features.

- **ETL Pipeline Design:** Build robust Extract, Transform, Load (ETL) pipelines tailored to ML needs. Focus on efficient data extraction, thorough transformation processes, and optimized loading strategies to ensure clean, well-structured data for analysis.

- **Data Quality Assurance:** Implement rigorous validation checks and data profiling throughout the ETL process to maintain data quality and consistency, which is crucial for accurate ML predictions.

- **Pipeline Optimization:** Continuously optimize data pipelines using techniques like incremental loading, parallel processing, and automation. Regularly measure performance and adjust strategies to handle evolving ML application demands.

CHAPTER 7

Model Training and Optimization

Training and optimizing ML models can feel like tackling a puzzle with countless moving pieces. The pursuit of efficiency and effectiveness in model training was never more exciting, especially when every tweak can unleash more power from your data. As ML systems become integral to our day-to-day applications, understanding the advanced techniques for model training and optimization becomes essential for anyone in the field. These practices not only speed up processes but also make model deployment smoother and more scalable across various projects.

With that said, let's dive into a blend of techniques that elevate model performance. We'll look into distributed training, where multiple machines work harmoniously to accelerate data processing, reducing time and effort significantly. Then there's hyperparameter tuning, which is all about finding that perfect balance in parameter settings that can transform average models into top performers. We'll also discuss transfer learning, a clever approach using pre-trained models to tackle new challenges without starting from scratch, and model compression, which focuses on keeping models efficient yet powerful. Each section brings unique insights and practical tips, arming you with the knowledge to enhance your ML prowess. It hardly matters if you're stepping into a new ML role or preparing for technical interviews; these strategies will give you a solid foundation and an edge in the ever-evolving tech landscape.

Distributed Training Techniques

Parallelizing model training across multiple machines is an important technique in accelerating ML processes, particularly when dealing with large datasets or complex models. Essentially, parallelization leverages the computational power of multiple machines to break down and process tasks more efficiently. This approach can significantly decrease training times and help manage the demands of modern AI applications. To implement this effectively, it's essential to understand two primary approaches: data parallelism and model parallelism.

Parallelizing Model Training Across Multiple Machines

Data parallelism involves splitting the dataset into smaller chunks that are then fed into separate instances of a model running on different machines. Each model instance processes a subset of the data, and the results are combined afterward. This method is especially beneficial for large datasets as it distributes the workload across multiple processors, making sure that no single machine becomes overwhelmed. In contrast, model parallelism divides the model itself across several machines. Each machine takes responsibility for computing specific parts of the model. This is particularly useful for very large models that cannot fit into the memory of a single machine. When leveraging both data and model parallelism, organizations can choose the method best suited to their needs based on the size of their data and models.

Frameworks and Tools for Distributed Training

There's a growing array of frameworks and tools designed specifically to facilitate efficient distributed training. Horovod and PyTorch Distributed are two popular examples. Horovod, developed by Uber, simplifies the process of adding data parallelism to existing ML models. It integrates seamlessly with many ML libraries and can significantly reduce training times without requiring substantial changes to the codebase. PyTorch Distributed, on the other hand, is a flexible tool within the PyTorch ecosystem that supports both data and model parallelism. It allows for fine-tuning of distributed training processes according to the specific needs of a project. These tools provide essential support in orchestrating distributed training, making the process smoother and more accessible for developers and engineers alike.

Challenges and Best Practices in Distributed ML Training

Despite these advancements, distributed training environments come with their own set of challenges. One major issue is synchronization. When multiple machines work on a model simultaneously, you have to make sure that consistency between updates becomes critical. Delays or mismatches in timing can lead to inefficient training and even erroneous results. Another challenge is network bandwidth. As machines communicate to share updates, limited bandwidth can become a bottleneck, slowing down the training process overall. Memory management also poses difficulties since each machine has finite resources, and mismanagement can lead to crashes or slowdowns. Furthermore, debugging distributed systems is often more complex than single-machine setups, requiring specialized techniques to diagnose and address issues effectively.

In order to maximize the efficiency of distributed training, there are several best practices that one should follow:

- **Consider the Architecture:** First of all, it's essential to carefully consider the architecture being used; choosing the right balance between data parallelism and model parallelism can have a significant impact on performance.

- **Use Profiling Tools:** These can offer insights into which parts of a model are most resource-intensive, guiding decisions on how to partition workloads most effectively.

- **Optimizing Communication Patterns:** Optimizing communication patterns between machines is vital. When you reduce unnecessary communication and aggregate updates intelligently, you can alleviate network strain and speed up training times. Additionally, adaptive learning rate strategies can be employed to account for variability in processing speeds across different machines.

- **Checkpointing:** Regularly saving the state of a model during training allows progress to be lost in the event of machine failures. This practice safeguards against data loss and allows for easier experimentation and iteration, as different configurations or hyperparameters can be tested without starting from scratch each time. Keeping an eye on system health and performance metrics provides valuable feedback. This helps in proactively addressing issues before they escalate, thereby maintaining smooth operations throughout the training period.

- **Collaborative Environment:** One last thing is to foster a collaborative environment among team members since it can enhance learning and innovation. Sharing knowledge and experiences, such as successful strategies and common pitfalls, contributes to a culture of continuous improvement. As more organizations adopt distributed training methods, the community's collective wisdom grows, ultimately leading to improved practices and technologies.

Introduction to Hyperparameter Tuning

Optimizing model hyperparameters can feel intricate. You've got parameters to tweak and results to evaluate, all while trying to keep the computational cost down. One way to bring some order to this chaos is through automated methods of hyperparameter optimization. Let's take a closer look at a few strategies that can help you find the sweet spot for your ML models.

Different Techniques

Grid search is one of the most straightforward methods available. It operates by exhaustively searching over a specified parameter grid. Say that you lay out all possible combinations of your parameters on a grid, then test each combination to see how well they perform. For those who love structure, grid search provides a neat and organized way to go about parameter exploration. However, it's worth noting that it's not always the most efficient, especially if you're dealing with high-dimensional space or large datasets. The computational cost can quickly add up as the number of evaluated points increases, making it essential to balance thoroughness with resource constraints.

Random Search

If grid search seems too demanding on your resources, random search offers a more flexible alternative. Rather than evaluating every single point on the grid, random search selects random combinations of parameters to test. While this might sound haphazard, it's surprisingly effective for broader exploration with reduced computational expense. Random search is particularly useful in scenarios where certain parameters have less influence on the outcome, allowing more focus on those that do. This means that, by randomly sampling points in the search space, there's a higher chance of stumbling upon good parameter sets sooner than grid search might.

Bayesian Optimization

Now, let's turn to Bayesian optimization, which takes things a step further by incorporating probabilistic models to guide the search process. This method is adept at capturing complex relationships between hyperparameters and model performance, leading to more informed and purposeful exploration. Bayesian optimization constructs a surrogate model of the performance function and uses it to predict the outcomes of different combinations. With this predictive power, the search process becomes significantly more efficient, focusing efforts on regions of the search space that are more likely to yield improvements.

Hyperparameter Optimization

Balancing computational cost with improved accuracy is the tightrope every data scientist or ML engineer must walk. Hyperparameter optimization's goal is to enhance model performance, yet it should also consider the computational overhead involved. Automated methods like those described allow practitioners to allocate resources wisely, optimizing for both speed and precision. Using an approach that aligns with your project's specific needs can make all the difference—whether prioritizing reduced time, lower costs, or increased accuracy.

Which Method to Choose?

Choosing the right method depends largely on your project's unique demands. If complete coverage of parameter combinations is critical, grid search could be your go-to. Meanwhile, if you're aiming for efficiency and equally good results, random search offers a compelling option without the burden of testing every possibility. And for those tackling complex problems where interactions between parameters aren't immediately clear, Bayesian optimization can be transformative, bringing clarity and focus to what might otherwise be a daunting task.

In practice, combining these methods can also be beneficial. For instance, starting with a random search can help identify promising regions in your search space efficiently. Once you've narrowed down the possibilities, switching to Bayesian optimization allows for fine-tuning within those regions, leveraging its strength in modeling parameter interactions. This hybrid approach can harness the strengths of each method, ultimately achieving balanced performance improvement without unnecessary expenditure of computational resources.

Real-Life Scenarios

Let's imagine a practical scenario: You're training a neural network to classify images. Initially, you employ grid search to explore several key hyperparameters like learning rate, batch size, and number of hidden layers. As the dimensionality grows, the sheer volume of potential combinations makes grid search cumbersome and time-prohibitive. That's when a shift to random search proves worthwhile. When exploring random combinations, you swiftly identify configurations that yield satisfactory results without exhausting your computing budget.

Suppose you reach a stage where performance gains become marginal. This situation calls for Bayesian optimization. Leveraging its ability to model complex interactions and predict beneficial hyperparameter settings, you zero in on the optimal configuration with relatively fewer evaluations. If you understand the trade-offs among these methods, you can make informed decisions that align with both technical goals and resource limitations.

Ultimately, successful hyperparameter tuning is a blend of art and science. Automated methods offer varying degrees of rigor and insight, allowing ML practitioners to optimize their models effectively. Whether you're a software engineer transitioning into the field, a data scientist preparing for technical interviews, or a fresh graduate eager to break into the industry, familiarizing yourself with these strategies will deepen your understanding of crafting robust, efficient models.

Transfer Learning and Fine-Tuning

Leveraging pre-trained models is a powerful strategy for ML practitioners. The concept here involves taking a model trained on a large dataset and adapting it, or fine-tuning it, to perform well on a different, often smaller, task-specific dataset. This approach can save an enormous amount of time and computational resources. Imagine you're working with a pre-trained image recognition model from a vast dataset like ImageNet. When fine-tuning this model on images specific to your field, such as medical scans, you can achieve excellent performance without needing to start training from scratch.

Techniques for Fine-Tuning Models on Domain-Specific Data

Fine-tuning is a bit of an art. It's not just about plugging in your new data and hitting the train button. You need to consider which layers to freeze and which to adjust, depending on how similar your domain-specific dataset is to the original one. If you're dealing with images that are quite similar to those in the initial dataset, you might only retrain the final layers. On the other hand, if there's a big difference, more extensive retraining could be necessary. A good practice is to start by freezing most of the layers and gradually unfreezing them through trial and error until you find what works best.

Transfer Learning in Computer Vision and Natural Language Processes

When it comes to transfer learning, the two fields where it shines brightest are computer vision and natural language processing (NLP). Take computer vision: Using models like ResNet or VGG, which have learned extremely rich feature representations, you can tailor these capabilities to tasks like identifying plant diseases or detecting vehicles in traffic images with minimal new data. In NLP, models such as BERT or GPT have drastically changed how we approach tasks like sentiment analysis or language translation. They allow for simple tweaks to adapt to specific dialects or subject matter while maintaining the depth learned from vast text corpora.

Challenges and Considerations in Applying Transfer Learning

However, the road to effective transfer learning isn't all smooth. One common pitfall is handling overfitting, especially when your target dataset is small. Overfitting occurs when your model is too closely tailored to the training data, capturing noise rather than signal. Regularization techniques and careful cross-validation can help mitigate this risk. Another challenge is dataset discrepancy, where differences in quality or distribution between the pre-trained and new datasets can negatively impact performance. Techniques like domain adaptation can be explored to realign these discrepancies, ensuring the model generalizes better to the new task.

When applying transfer learning, we also need to tread carefully concerning ethical considerations and potential biases. Models pre-trained on large datasets may inadvertently carry over biases present in the original data. If a model trained predominantly on Western-centric data is used for applications in vastly different cultural settings, the results might perpetuate unfair outcomes. It's important to scrutinize the origin of your pre-trained models and actively seek diverse datasets for further training. This allows for the adapted models to serve all users fairly and equitably.

Also, understanding the social environment in which these models operate is vital. Take facial recognition systems as an example; if they are primarily trained on one demographic and then applied globally, this can lead to biased outputs. To counteract these issues, it's important to include representative samples from all user groups in fine-tuning processes. This kind of ethical diligence helps prevent technology from becoming a tool for reinforcing societal disparities.

Challenges and Best Practices in Model Optimization

When optimizing ML models, a key challenge is addressing overfitting and underfitting. These phenomena occur when a model either learns too much about the training data or too little to generalize well to new data.

What Is Overfitting?

Overfitting happens when a model captures noise along with the underlying patterns, which leads to high accuracy on training data but poor performance on testing data. Techniques such as regularization, dropout, and early stopping can help mitigate overfitting. Regularization is about adding a penalty term to the model's loss function to keep the learned weights small. Dropout randomly sets some neurons to zero during training, preventing co-adaptation of hidden units. Early stopping monitors the model's performance on a validation set and halts training if the performance begins to degrade.

What Is Underfitting?

Underfitting, on the other hand, occurs when a model is too simple to capture complex patterns in the data, resulting in poor predictions across both the training and test datasets. Increasing the complexity of the model by adding more layers in a neural network, increasing the number of parameters, or selecting more sophisticated algorithms can help overcome underfitting. Providing the model with more diverse and representative data can enhance its ability to learn meaningful patterns.

Considerations in Model Optimization

Another major consideration in model optimization is confronting the computational costs associated with both the training and inference phases.

Training Models

Training large-scale models needs significant computational resources, which can be costly and time-consuming. Strategies for reducing this burden include using hardware accelerators like GPUs or TPUs, which are specially designed to handle the vast calculations needed for training deep learning models efficiently. Implementing techniques like mini-batch gradient descent instead of batch gradient descent can also contribute to faster convergence by updating model weights incrementally based on subsets of the training data rather than the entire dataset.

Inference Phase

Beyond training, the inference phase can pose its own set of challenges. Real-time applications require models that not only predict accurately but do so swiftly. Quantization and pruning are effective methods to reduce model size for faster inference. Quantization reduces the precision of the numbers (weights and activations) within a model, while pruning removes unnecessary weights, simplifying the model structure without significantly compromising accuracy.

Optimizing ML models isn't a one-time task but an ongoing process that demands systematic approaches to evaluate and refine model performance regularly. Cross-validation remains a fundamental technique in assessing how the statistical analysis will generalize to an independent dataset. The k-fold cross-validation method divides the dataset into k subsets or folds, making sure that every instance of the dataset has a chance of being included in the training and test set. This technique minimizes bias and variance, aiding in fine-tuning models for optimal performance.

Also, metrics such as accuracy, precision, recall, F1 score, and AUC-ROC curve are vital for comprehensive evaluation. It's essential to pick appropriate evaluation metrics based on the specific problem you're tackling. For classification tasks, the confusion matrix provides insights into true positives, false negatives, true negatives, and false positives, guiding adjustments in model parameters or architecture.

Continuous Monitoring and Iterative Adjustments

Continuous monitoring and iterative adjustments are indispensable for sustained model success. ML models operate in dynamic environments where data distributions frequently change, known as concept drift. Setting up automated monitoring systems to track model predictions can alert engineers to shifts requiring intervention. Automated retraining pipelines allow models to adapt by incorporating new data, maintaining relevance and accuracy over time.

In implementing continuous monitoring, tools like MLflow, TensorBoard, and Neptune enable tracking model experiments, logging results, and visualizing performance metrics. By doing so, stakeholders can easily analyze trends, diagnose issues, and optimize workflows systematically. Iterative adjustments might involve retuning hyperparameters, modifying the model architecture, or updating the feature engineering pipeline to accommodate newly discovered patterns.

Establishing a feedback loop that integrates real-world performance can also uncover areas of improvement not previously considered. Engaging domain experts for qualitative insights and leveraging user interactions through A/B testing are practical approaches to refine models iteratively. Importantly, fostering a culture where experimental changes are encouraged helps teams remain agile and innovative in their optimization efforts.

Quizzes and Exercises

Quiz

1. What is distributed training in machine learning, and why is it important for large-scale models?

2. Explain the difference between data parallelism and model parallelism in distributed training.

3. Name two popular frameworks or tools used for distributed training in ML.

4. What are the main challenges in implementing distributed ML training?

5. Define hyperparameter tuning and explain its importance in model optimization.

Exercises

1. **Distributed Training Implementation:** Design a distributed training setup for a large-scale image classification model using a framework of your choice (such as PyTorch Distributed, or Horovod). Outline the key components of your setup, including data distribution, model synchronization, and communication between nodes. Discuss potential bottlenecks and how you would address them.

2. **Hyperparameter Tuning Experiment:** Choose a publicly available dataset and a machine learning algorithm (like a random forest, neural network). Implement grid search, random search, and

Bayesian optimization for hyperparameter tuning. Compare the results in terms of model performance and computational efficiency. Present your findings and discuss which method you would recommend for different scenarios.

3. **Distributed vs. Non-Distributed Training Comparison:** Conduct an experiment comparing the training time and model performance of a non-distributed training approach versus a distributed approach for a moderately sized neural network. Use a public dataset of your choice. Present your results, including training times, model accuracies, and resource use. Discuss the trade-offs between the two approaches.

Key Insights and Practical Takeaways

- **Distributed Training:** Leverage techniques like data parallelism and model parallelism to accelerate training across multiple machines. Use frameworks like Horovod or PyTorch Distributed to implement distributed training efficiently.

- **Hyperparameter Tuning:** Employ automated methods such as grid search, random search, or Bayesian optimization to find optimal model parameters. Choose the method based on your project's specific needs and computational resources.

- **Transfer Learning:** Use pre-trained models and fine-tune them for domain-specific tasks to save time and resources. Be mindful of potential biases in pre-trained models and ensure ethical considerations are addressed.

- **Model Optimization:** Address overfitting and underfitting using techniques like regularization, dropout, and early stopping. Implement strategies to reduce computational costs during both training and inference phases, such as using hardware accelerators or model compression techniques.

- **Continuous Monitoring:** Establish automated monitoring systems and feedback loops to track model performance over time. Regularly evaluate and refine models using appropriate metrics and techniques like cross-validation to maintain relevance and accuracy in dynamic environments.

CHAPTER 8

ML Model Deployment Strategies

Sure, deploying ML models is just about making them work. However, it's also about making sure they run smoothly and predictably in real-world settings. Imagine building a model that's like your favorite recipe; it's perfect when you make it at home, but how do you ensure it turns out the same every time, whether you're at your friend's house or on a TV cooking show? This chapter goes into that exact predicament of model deployment, exploring the variety of strategies one can use to seamlessly integrate ML models into production environments.

Here, expect to explore the intricacies of containerization with tools like Docker, which pack up all your model's bits and pieces for reliable travel across different setups. We'll unravel the mysteries of orchestration using Kubernetes, helping manage these containers at scale and making sure they work together gracefully without tripping over each other. Beyond just getting models into the world, we'll also talk about testing strategies, such as A/B testing, that let you experiment with different model versions to find the best performer. Finally, we'll walk through various deployment architectures, comparing frameworks and solutions tailored to meet specific needs, ensuring you have the knowledge to choose the right tool for the job.

Containerization and Orchestration

In ML, deploying models efficiently and reliably is just as important as everything else we mentioned before. This is where containerization plays a vital role, which serves as a key solution for packaging ML models in a standardized manner. Think of Docker as your model's travel suitcase—it neatly holds all necessary files, libraries, and dependencies, knowing that whatever environment you deploy it to, the setup remains consistent. This consistency is vital because it prevents the dreaded "it works on my machine" syndrome from arising when code behaves differently across different infrastructures.

Using Docker for Containerizing ML Models

Now, let's go into using Docker for this purpose. If you place your ML models into Docker containers, you create portable units that are easy to share, replicate, and deploy across various environments. These containers can run uniformly whether you're testing locally on a laptop or deploying to a cloud service halfway around the globe. This uniformity simplifies deployment and streamlines collaboration among teams, as everyone can work with the same containerized application, avoiding version mismatches or configuration issues.

Orchestrating With Kubernetes for Managing ML Deployments

Once you've packaged your models in containers, the next challenge is managing them efficiently, especially at scale. Enter Kubernetes—a powerful tool for orchestrating containerized applications across clusters of machines. Kubernetes automates many operational tasks, such as deploying, scaling, and managing containers in clustered environments, turning complex deployments into more manageable processes. Picture Kubernetes as the traffic controller of your container highway, directing incoming and outgoing containers to make sure there are smooth operations without any bottlenecks or crashes.

With Kubernetes, you gain the ability to monitor your applications' health actively. It provides self-healing capabilities, automatically restarting failed containers and replacing them with healthier versions. This means increased uptime and reliability for your ML models, which is critical when they form part of a production system that must be available 24/7. Moreover, Kubernetes allows for horizontal scaling by distributing workloads evenly, making sure resources are used effectively according to demand.

Creating Reproducible ML Environments

While the benefits of containerizing and orchestrating ML models are clear, creating reproducible ML environments is another layer that greatly enhances reliability and control. Reproducibility allows models to perform predictably no matter how often they're deployed. This has to do with maintaining control over software dependencies and versioning throughout development and deployment cycles. If you use consistent base images for Docker containers, these can easily manage run-time dependencies, while tagging version-controlled images helps revert back to previous states if needed. This approach minimizes discrepancies that could arise from differing library versions or incompatible updates.

Best Practices for Containerizing Different Types of ML Models

However, effective containerization goes beyond just setting up Docker and Kubernetes. Implementing best practices can optimize your deployment strategy significantly. One aspect is optimizing image sizes. Smaller images mean faster uploads, downloads, and deployments, which translate to reduced start-up times and lower bandwidth usage. You can achieve this by only including essential components in your images, thereby reducing their overall footprint. Use multi-stage builds to separate build-time dependencies from run-time ones, thus shrinking final image sizes.

Resource management is another important consideration. Containers should be allocated sufficient CPU and memory resources to function optimally, but not so much that other applications suffer. Kubernetes makes resource allocation easier through namespaces and resource quotas, allowing you to define limits to prevent any single container from consuming too much of the cluster's resources.

Network security within containerized systems also deserves special attention. As containers become integral parts of your infrastructure, protecting them against vulnerabilities becomes essential. Make sure that only approved and trusted images are used by scanning for vulnerabilities regularly and implementing policies to deny risky images. Additionally, employing network policies to restrict container communications can safeguard sensitive data from unauthorized access.

Introduction to A/B Testing

A/B testing is a valuable tool in the arsenal of any ML professional aiming to optimize model performance. Its primary goal is to validate ML models in real-world scenarios by comparing different versions to see which performs better. Think of it as a scientific experiment for evaluating your models, helping you understand their effectiveness before full deployment.

Implementing A/B Testing for ML Models

The process begins with implementing A/B testing, where two or more versions of an ML model are compared. For example, you might tweak algorithms, features, or preprocessing methods between versions. Imagine releasing Model A with one set of features and Model B with another. When presenting both versions to users under controlled conditions, you can gather data on their performance. This side-by-side comparison provides insights into how modifications impact metrics like accuracy, recall, or user satisfaction. A/B tests allow you to decide if changes truly enhance model performance or if they introduce unforeseen issues.

However, designing effective A/B tests is important to obtaining reliable results. You must allow statistical significance, minimizing biases that could skew outcomes. To achieve this, clear objectives and hypotheses must be defined, followed by allocating sufficient sample sizes. Consider using randomization techniques to assign users to different model versions, reducing selection bias. With appropriate sample sizes and randomness, you're more likely to discern genuine improvements over noise. Remember, the goal is to derive conclusions that reflect genuine user interactions with the models rather than anomalies.

Once your A/B test is underway, analyzing the results becomes a crucial step. It's not just about tallying winners or losers; instead, it focuses on understanding why certain models outperform others. Dive deep into user behavior and engagement patterns. If Model B shows higher conversion rates or retention, identify what changes contributed to those outcomes. Were there specific segments of users who reacted differently? Such insights allow you to iterate intelligently, tailoring models for diverse user needs.

This analysis should feed directly into decision-making processes regarding model improvements or deployments. Rather than blindly pushing updates, use evidence from A/B testing to guide these actions. If a model version demonstrates superior performance, consider scaling it up gradually. On the other hand, if results reveal shortcomings, it's an opportunity to revisit assumptions and refine algorithms. The iterative nature of A/B testing aligns seamlessly with the continuous development journey of ML models, promoting ongoing refinement and excellence.

To effectively evaluate A/B test results, determining appropriate metrics and key performance indicators (KPIs) is essential. These metrics can be used as a compass for interpreting outcomes. While standard metrics like accuracy or precision are valuable, they may not encompass the entire story. For example, an ML-based recommendation system might prioritize click-through rates or time spent on recommended content. Tailor your KPIs to align with business goals and user experiences. This approach allows for that model's success to translates into meaningful benefits for end-users and stakeholders alike.

Keep in mind that different contexts require different KPIs. A financial decision-support model might focus on reducing false positives, while a healthcare application might emphasize sensitivity and specificity. When you pick relevant KPIs, you gain a comprehensive understanding of how well each model version meets its intended purpose. Also, communicating these insights clearly within your team fosters informed discussions and strategic planning.

The iterative cycle of refining models based on A/B testing creates a culture of constant improvement within ML teams. Embrace these learnings to drive future developments, exploring innovative ways to enhance model capabilities. Encouraged collaboration among cross-functional teams, including data scientists, software engineers, and product managers, also enriches this process. Diverse perspectives contribute to robust solutions, preventing tunnel vision that might arise from isolated analysis.

Model Serving Architectures

When getting into the world of model-serving frameworks, it's essential to understand their role in deploying ML models effectively and efficiently. Two popular frameworks that often come up in discussions are TensorFlow Serving and MLflow. Each offers unique features tailored to different deployment needs, but understanding their strengths and limitations will help you decide which framework suits your projects best.

Comparing Different Model Serving Frameworks

TensorFlow Serving: This framework is designed specifically to serve TensorFlow models, offering a robust solution for production environments. It provides out-of-the-box support for versioned models, facilitating easy updates without interrupting service. Its focus on performance means it excels in situations requiring high throughput and low latency—ideal for real-time applications such as recommendation systems or fraud detection. However, its specialization in TensorFlow can be a limitation if you're working with models developed in other frameworks, potentially leading to compatibility issues.

MLflow: On the other hand, MLflow shines with its flexibility. It's an open-source platform that is not limited to one specific framework and supports various tools and languages across the ML lifecycle. MLflow's model-serving feature allows you to take any model and deploy it as a REST API, making it extremely versatile. This cross-framework support makes it perfect if your workflow involves multiple platforms. However, this flexibility might require additional setup and configuration, which could be a barrier for those seeking out-of-the-box solutions.

Designing Scalable Architectures for High-Throughput Model Serving

Designing scalable architectures that handle high-throughput requirements with low latency is important in real-time ML applications. These architectures should be capable of processing large volumes of requests efficiently while ensuring minimal delay in response time. One strategy is to implement asynchronous processing where applicable. When decoupling the incoming data processing from the request-response cycle, you can reduce latency and improve responsiveness. Employing caching mechanisms for frequently accessed data or predictions can further optimize response times, ensuring your system meets stringent real-time requirements.

Scalability for High-Throughput Model Serving

Scalability is a critical consideration in the deployment of ML models, particularly when demand surges or spikes occur. Techniques like load balancing and distributed computing become invaluable in such scenarios. Load balancing distributes incoming traffic evenly across servers or instances, which prevents any single point of failure and allows consistent performance under heavy loads. Distributed computing, meanwhile, allows computation to be spread across a network of computers, leveraging additional resources for enhanced processing power. When implementing these techniques, you prepare your architecture to gracefully scale with increasing demands without compromising on performance.

System Robustness in High-Throughput Model Serving

Ensuring system robustness is another essential aspect, requiring the implementation of fault-tolerant mechanisms and continuous monitoring of serve performance. Fault tolerance involves designing systems that continue functioning even when components fail. This robustness is achieved through redundancy and failover strategies, where backup systems automatically take over in case of failures, minimizing downtime. Continuous monitoring increases this by allowing real-time insights into system health and performance metrics. Tools like Prometheus or Grafana can be employed to set up dashboards and alerts, providing an early warning system for potential issues that need attention.

Combining all these elements forms a comprehensive approach to deploying ML models efficiently and reliably. Picking the right model serving framework depends on your specific needs and existing infrastructure. While TensorFlow Serving might be more suited for environments heavily invested in TensorFlow workflows, MLflow provides broader applicability across diverse setups.

Designing for scalability addresses both current and future needs, accommodating growth and fluctuating workloads with ease. Load balancing and distributed computing allows your application to remain responsive and available, regardless of user demand or volume. When building robust systems equipped with fault-tolerance and monitoring tools, you safeguard against unexpected disruptions, maintaining service continuity and quality.

Incorporating guidelines on designing scalable architectures can provide clarity and direction. For instance, assess the peak load your application might experience and plan your resources accordingly. Implement automation for scaling so that your system can adjust resource allocation dynamically. Also, geographic distribution for global applications should be considered to reduce latency and balance load across regions.

Chapter Quiz and Exercises

Quiz

1. What are the main benefits of using containerization for ML model deployment?

2. Explain the role of Kubernetes in orchestrating ML model deployments.

3. What are some best practices for creating reproducible ML environments using containers?

4. How does containerization differ for different types of ML models (like deep learning models vs. classical ML models)?

5. What is A/B testing in the context of ML model deployment, and why is it important?

Exercises

1. **Docker Containerization:** Choose an ML model of your choice. Create a Dockerfile that encapsulates the model and its dependencies. Explain each step in your Dockerfile and discuss how it contributes to creating a reproducible environment.

2. **Kubernetes Deployment:** Design a Kubernetes deployment configuration for an ML model serving application. Include considerations for scaling, resource allocation, and high availability. Explain your configuration choices and how they address potential challenges in ML model deployment.

3. **A/B Testing Strategy:** Develop an A/B testing strategy for deploying a new version of a recommendation system model. Outline the steps you would take to set up the test, including how you would split traffic, what metrics you would monitor, and how you would determine the success of the new model. Discuss potential pitfalls and how to avoid them.

Key Insights and Practical Takeaways

- **Containerization:** Use Docker to package ML models with their dependencies, ensuring consistency across different environments and simplifying deployment processes.

- **Orchestration:** Implement Kubernetes for managing containerized ML deployments at scale, automating tasks like scaling and monitoring container health.

- **A/B Testing:** Employ A/B testing to compare different model versions in real-world scenarios, using appropriate metrics and sample sizes to make data-driven decisions on model improvements.

- **Model Serving Frameworks:** Choose between frameworks like TensorFlow Serving and MLflow based on your specific needs, considering factors such as model compatibility and deployment flexibility.

- **Scalable Architecture:** Design for high-throughput and low-latency by implementing techniques like load balancing, distributed computing, and asynchronous processing to handle increasing demands efficiently.

BOOK 2

Advanced Machine Learning System Design

CHAPTER 9

Deep Learning Systems

Designing and implementing deep learning systems is very exciting, especially when it comes to AI. These systems, which include intricate architectures like neural networks, have transformed how we approach tasks ranging from image recognition to natural language processing. At the heart of these transformative technologies are the neural network architectures that serve as building blocks for powerful AI models. Understanding these structures opens the door to mastering deep learning's potential, enabling us to harness its capabilities for various innovative applications. The selection and configuration of these networks are central to achieving optimal performance, which makes this a key area of focus for anyone looking to get deeper into ML.

In this chapter, we will talk about neural network architectures, going further into their designs and implementations. You'll learn about the popular types, such as CNNs, RNNs, and Transformers, each with unique strengths and use cases. We'll touch on the challenges of scaling these models and the hardware considerations that have a vital role in their deployment. Going into these topics will give you practical insights, whether you're aiming to transition into an ML role, improve your understanding of system design principles, or prepare for those technical interviews. When examining these foundational elements, you'll be better prepared to navigate the complex world of deep learning and apply these concepts effectively in real-world scenarios.

Neural Network Architectures

When it comes to deep learning systems, there's an elaborate array of neural network architectures to choose from. Let's go into some of the most popular ones—CNNs, RNNs, and Transformers—and understand their unique features and applications.

Convolutional Neural Networks

CNNs are particularly well-suited for analyzing visual imagery. CNNs excel in identifying and leveraging spatial hierarchies in data, making them indispensable in tasks like image recognition or object detection. They operate through a series of convolutional layers, each extracting increasingly complex features from the input images. This architecture has made tremendous strides in fields such as autonomous vehicles and medical diagnostics, where precise image interpretation is important.

Recurrent Neural Networks

RNNs are customized for sequential data analysis. Their capacity to process sequences by maintaining a "memory" of previous inputs makes them suitable for tasks involving time series data, such as language modeling and speech recognition. Despite their strength, RNNs face challenges with long-term dependencies due to vanishing gradient problems, which has led to the development of more sophisticated variants like LSTM and GRU networks. These advances keep RNNs relevant in NLP and other sequential prediction tasks.

Transformers

Transformers have come up as a groundbreaking architecture, revolutionizing NLP through their ability to handle long-range dependencies without recourse to recurrent connections. When you employ mechanisms like self-attention, transformers efficiently focus on different parts of an input sequence when predicting outputs, which makes them highly effective in machine translation, text generation, and beyond. With models like BERT and GPT, transformers have set new benchmarks in understanding context and nuance in textual data.

Designing Custom Neural Network Architectures for Specific Tasks

Designing custom neural network architectures encompasses a creative yet methodical approach. The goal is often to tailor these models to specific tasks while balancing adaptability and specificity. It starts with understanding the problem domain: what are the expected inputs and desired outputs? Once defined, engineers can determine whether existing architectures suffice or if there's a need for customization, which could involve combining elements from various architectures or introducing novel layers to capture task-specific features.

Designing Custom Architectures

Guidelines for designing custom architectures emphasize iterative experimentation and adjustment. Using tools like AutoML can expedite the process by automating model selection and hyperparameter tuning, but manual tweaks are often necessary to fine-tune performance. It's important to maintain adaptability, allowing the model to adjust to new data patterns while ensuring it remains focused enough to avoid overfitting irrelevant features.

The Balance Between Model Complexity and Performance

This is a trade-off that echoes throughout deep learning system design. On one end of the spectrum, simpler models may execute faster and consume fewer resources. However, they might fall short in capturing intricate data patterns, thus compromising accuracy. On the other hand, overly complex models might deliver superior accuracy, but at the expense of increased computational costs and extended training times. This can be particularly problematic when scaling up systems for production environments.

Striking the right balance calls for a keen assessment of priorities—be it accuracy, computational efficiency, or resource consumption. For example, in scenarios where real-time predictions are imperative, like automated trading systems or live captioning services, prioritizing speed and efficiency over raw accuracy may be warranted. Alternatively, in fields like scientific research, where precision trumps all, complex models might be justified despite their cost.

Best Practices in Neural Network Design and Implementation

When implementing best practices in neural network design, practical considerations align closely with real-world constraints and objectives. A pertinent best practice is about regular cross-validation, ensuring that models are neither overfitted nor underperforming on unseen data. Engineers are encouraged to adopt modular design approaches, enabling components to be updated or replaced without overhauling entire systems. This flexibility is relevant as new techniques and architectures are created.

Also, leveraging techniques such as dropout, batch normalization, and learning rate scheduling can improve robustness and convergence rates during training. Ensuring these models are interpretable, also enables engineers and stakeholders to grasp decision-making processes, promoting trust and facilitating debugging.

Managing and optimizing resource allocation are quite important. Efficient usage of hardware accelerators like GPUs or TPUs can drastically reduce training times and improve throughput, especially when dealing with large datasets or intricate models. Employing cloud-based solutions for scalable infrastructure also allows teams to adapt swiftly to changing demands without significant upfront investments.

Training at Scale

Training large-scale deep learning models is quite a challenge, full of complexities that require strategic approaches. One of the primary challenges lies in the sheer computational power and data management these models demand. Deep learning models grow with layers and parameters, making them resource-hungry monsters that can easily overwhelm even robust systems. These models need immense processing capabilities to execute numerous calculations simultaneously. Handling and organizing vast amounts of data for training without hitting bottlenecks is another significant concern. Efficient computation is relevant to make sure operations run smoothly and effectively.

Challenges in Training Large-Scale Deep Learning Models

To tackle these demands, exploring distributed training strategies becomes very important. Distributed training allows us to spread tasks across multiple processors or machines, thus enhancing efficiency and scalability. In this arena, data parallelism and model parallelism offer distinct advantages. Data parallelism is all about distributing different segments of the dataset to various computing resources, allowing simultaneous processing and remarkably reducing training time. It's like having multiple chefs working on different parts of a big meal, each contributing to the final dish concurrently. Alternatively, model parallelism divides the model's computations itself, splitting the network across various devices. Each device handles a different chunk of the model, facilitating simultaneous computations and thus, improving scalability. These strategies are critical for anyone looking to optimize training for extensive deep learning networks.

Optimizing Memory Usage and Computational Efficiency

Memory optimization: This is another key area when dealing with large models, as it helps prevent system overloads. Techniques such as gradient checkpointing can be particularly useful. Gradient checkpointing saves memory by selectively storing certain data points during backpropagation rather than all activations, which eases the memory burden considerably. Also, using mixed precision training, where some calculations are done with lower precision, can significantly boost performance while conserving memory usage. This approach reduces memory requirements and increases computational speed without compromising accuracy. Employing these techniques allows memory capacity to not become a bottleneck, enabling models to train effectively despite their size.

Managing large datasets: To manage this efficiently is absolutely crucial for successful model training. Effective data preprocessing has an important role here, transforming raw data into a cleaner format suitable for feeding into models. Properly preprocessed data can prevent potential issues during training and improve overall model effectiveness. Sharding datasets, which involves dividing them into smaller, manageable parts, is another practical tactic. This method allows for more efficient use of storage and faster data retrieval times, ensuring smoother training processes. Constructing efficient data pipelines helps maintain a continuous flow of data to the model during training. These pipelines automate the data journey from raw form through preprocessing to being fed into the model, saving considerable time and effort while boosting efficiency.

Deployment Challenges

Deploying deep learning models in production environments is a complex yet crucial aspect of modern AI applications. This task needs to address several challenges to ensure that these models can perform reliable and efficient operations at a large scale. The journey begins with understanding best practices for serving models within production settings, where reliability and low latency are key.

Serving Deep Learning Models in Production Environments

When you're deploying models at scale, the process is more than just transferring your model from development to production. It's about ensuring that each request is processed quickly and efficiently, maintaining robust performance under varying loads. One approach to achieving this is through load balancing and horizontal scaling, which allow multiple instances of a model to handle requests concurrently, reducing latency and preventing bottlenecks.

Another critical component in serving models is the use of caching mechanisms. Caching repeated inference requests can significantly speed up response times. Tools like TensorFlow Serving or NVIDIA Triton Inference Server provide frameworks to manage these demands effectively, leveraging GPU acceleration and optimizing inference pipelines.

Handling Updates and Versioning for Deep Learning Systems

Managing model updates and versioning is another challenge that can't be overlooked. Models must evolve over time: data drifts, new features are added, and algorithms improve. This evolution needs a systematic approach to update management. Implementing A/B testing or canary releases can help smoothly transition between model versions, ensuring that updates don't disrupt existing services.

Version control systems, much like those used in software development, are essential here. They enable you to track changes in model code, parameters, and data dependencies. Such systems increase reproducibility and accountability, relevant aspects when dealing with frequently updated models.

Optimizing Inference Speed for Real-Time Applications

Optimizing inference speed, especially in real-time applications, requires a strategic focus.

Inference speed: This directly impacts user experience in scenarios like recommendation systems, autonomous vehicles, or financial trading platforms. One strategy is model quantization—reducing the precision of model weights and activations—which can lead to faster computations without significant loss in accuracy.

Pruning: This is yet another effective technique. When you remove redundant neurons and connections, you streamline the model's architecture, sometimes halving the computational load. Combining these techniques with hardware acceleration—leveraging GPUs and TPUs for parallel processing—can drastically cut down response times.

Monitoring and Debugging Deep Learning Models in Production

Monitoring and debugging post-deployment are fundamental to sustaining performance and reliability.

Monitoring: Once a model is live, it enters an ever-changing environment, subject to data shifts and operational anomalies. Continuous monitoring helps detect these issues early. Tools such as Prometheus, Grafana, and ELK Stack are invaluable for logging and visualizing system metrics.

Debugging deployed models: This often has to do with tracing back errors to specific input patterns or anomalies and needs detailed logs of inference activities. Plus, incorporating feedback loops enables active learning, allowing models to adapt by retraining on newly gathered data, closing the loop between deployment and model improvement.

Hardware Acceleration (GPUs, TPUs)

In the landscape of deep learning, specialized hardware like GPUs (Graphics Processing Units) and TPUs (Tensor Processing Units) have become vital tools in unleashing the full potential of ML models. These technologies are specifically designed to handle the massive computational tasks required by deep learning algorithms, offering a significant boost in performance and efficiency compared to traditional CPUs.

Leveraging GPUs and TPUs for Deep Learning Computation

GPUs: These have long been the workhorses behind the rise of deep learning due to their ability to perform parallel processing efficiently. The nature of deep learning involves numerous matrix operations, which GPUs excel at handling concurrently. If distributing thousands of operations simultaneously across multiple cores, the GPUs significantly reduce the time required for training models, which makes them a staple in most deep learning projects today. However, it's important to know that your workload is optimized to make the most out of GPU capabilities. Properly managing memory allocation, using mixed precision training, and carefully structuring data pipelines are some strategies to avoid bottlenecks and improve performance.

TPUs: On the flip side, TPUs, developed by Google, are engineered specifically for ML tasks. They offer a custom architecture to accelerate tensor operations, providing further boosts in speed and efficiency over general-purpose GPUs. TPUs can execute complex neural network computations much faster by harnessing low-precision arithmetic operations, which simplifies calculations without compromising accuracy. Integrating TPUs into your workflow allows a nuanced understanding of their architecture, ensuring you align workload specifics with TPU strengths.

Optimizing Deep Learning Workloads for Specific Hardware

Beyond just having powerful hardware, optimizing workloads for these devices is vital. This optimization often involves adjusting model architectures, adapting batch sizes, and fine-tuning hyperparameters to fit the hardware's characteristics. For instance, using hardware-specific libraries or frameworks such as CUDA for GPUs or TensorFlow XLA for TPUs can significantly enhance the use of available resources. Also, leveraging software optimizations like pruning, quantization, and knowledge distillation can further maximize the cost-effectiveness and energy consumption of these high-performance machines.

Cloud vs. On-Premise Solutions for Deep Learning Computation

The decision between using cloud-based solutions or maintaining an on-premise setup presents another layer of consideration.

Cloud

Cloud providers, such as AWS, Google Cloud, and Azure, offer flexible, scalable infrastructures where you can rent powerful GPUs and TPUs. This option is particularly appealing for startups or smaller teams who need access to high-end hardware without substantial upfront investments. Cloud environments also provide seamless scaling, allowing organizations to handle fluctuating workloads efficiently. However, costs can escalate quickly, depending on usage patterns and data transfer requirements.

On-Premise

On-premise setups might be more suitable for larger enterprises looking to have complete control over their infrastructure. Owning your hardware allows for predictable costs and potentially increased security, as sensitive data remains within the organization's physical boundaries. However, it's important to consider the initial investment cost, ongoing maintenance, and the necessity of employing specialists to manage these systems. Infrastructure needs, scalability concerns, and security policies must be balanced to determine the most appropriate solution for deploying deep learning systems.

Emerging Hardware Technologies for AI Acceleration

While current hardware solutions are robust, the field of AI acceleration is far from static, with new technologies continuously promising paradigm shifts. Innovations like the introduction of neuromorphic chips, which mimic the human brain's neuronal structures, are poised to disrupt traditional processing methods by drastically increasing efficiency and power consumption. Similarly, the development of optical processors, which use light instead of electricity to perform computations, holds the potential to elevate data throughput and energy efficiency exponentially. Companies innovating in this space aim to push the boundaries of what's achievable with AI, driving future trends toward even faster and more efficient deep learning capabilities.

Quizzes and Exercises

Quiz

1. Compare and contrast CNNs, RNNs, and Transformers. In what types of tasks does each architecture excel?

2. What are the key considerations when designing a custom neural network architecture for a specific task?

3. Explain the trade-off between model complexity and performance in deep learning systems.

4. What are the main challenges in training large-scale deep learning models?

5. Describe two strategies for distributed training of deep neural networks.

Exercises

1. **Architecture Design:** Design a custom neural network architecture for a specific task of your choice (such as image segmentation, sentiment analysis, or time series forecasting). Explain your design choices, including the types of layers used, the overall structure, and any special components. Discuss the trade-offs you considered and how your architecture addresses the specific challenges of the chosen task.

2. **Distributed Training Implementation:** Implement a distributed training setup for a large-scale image classification model using a framework of your choice. Outline the key components of your setup, including data distribution, model synchronization, and communication between nodes. Discuss potential bottlenecks and how you would address them.

3. **Memory Optimization:** You're training a deep learning model on a dataset that doesn't fit in memory. Propose and implement three techniques to optimize memory usage during training. Compare the effectiveness of each technique in terms of memory savings and impact on training time.

Key Insights and Practical Takeaways

- **Neural Network Architectures:** Understand the strengths and applications of different architectures like CNNs (for visual data), RNNs (for sequential data), and Transformers (for NLP tasks). Choose the appropriate architecture based on your specific task requirements.

- **Custom Architecture Design:** Balance model complexity with performance when designing custom neural networks. Use techniques like AutoML for initial architecture selection, but be prepared to fine-tune manually for optimal results.

- **Distributed Training:** Implement distributed training strategies like data parallelism and model parallelism to handle large-scale deep learning models efficiently. This approach helps manage computational demands and improve scalability.

- **Hardware Acceleration:** Leverage GPUs and TPUs to accelerate deep learning computations. Optimize workloads for specific hardware using techniques like mixed precision training and efficient memory management to maximize performance.

- **Deployment Considerations:** Address challenges in serving models in production environments by implementing load balancing, caching mechanisms, and efficient versioning systems. Continuously monitor and debug deployed models to maintain performance and reliability.

CHAPTER 10

Natural Language Processing Systems

Designing and implementing NLP systems is like unraveling the complex strings of human language to teach machines how to understand and interact with text. It's a field where technology meets linguistics, creating a bridge between human communication and AI. In this chapter, we will go into the intricacies of NLP systems, exploring various tasks that these systems can accomplish and the challenges they face when dealing with language-based ML applications. For those venturing into this fascinating industry, it's all about harnessing the power of algorithms to decode meaning and context, turning raw data into structured information.

Throughout this chapter, we'll be mentioning essential components and techniques relevant to building effective NLP systems. From text classification to more advanced tasks like Named Entity Recognition (NER) and machine translation, each section presents an opportunity to understand how different methodologies are applied. You'll learn about the architectures, such as CNNs and RNNs, that underlie many text processing systems, the preprocessing techniques that clean and prepare data, and the feature extraction methods that turn text into quantifiable data. We also go into handling imbalanced datasets, an often-overlooked challenge in real-world applications, allowing your systems to remain accurate and unbiased.

Text Classification

In the world of NLP, text classification systems are a fundamental component that enables machines to understand and categorize vast amounts of textual data. Designing these systems encompasses several critical methodologies, starting with selecting the right architecture. Two popular choices are convolutional neural networks (CNNs) and recurrent neural networks (RNNs). CNNs are adept at capturing local features and identifying key patterns within chunks of text, making them highly effective for tasks where context is relatively confined. On the other hand, RNNs, with their ability to maintain context through sequential data, shine in tasks involving longer texts or documents where understanding dependencies between words across sentences is vital.

Architectures for Text Classification Tasks

Next, let's talk about preprocessing techniques, which are vital for preparing raw text data for classification. Tokenization is a foundational step that breaks down text into manageable pieces or tokens, such as words or phrases. When converting a document into a sequence of tokens, algorithms can more easily analyze the text. Stemming and lemmatization simplify tokens to their root forms, which helps standardize the input data and improve model performance. Removing stop-words—common words like "and," "the," and "is"—reduces noise in the dataset, allowing models to focus on meaningful terms that contribute more significantly to classification outcomes.

Preprocessing Techniques for Text Data

A few guidelines for preprocessing include making sure of consistent tokenization across your dataset and choosing stemming or lemmatization based on the complexity and nature of the text. Experimenting with different combinations can yield insights into what works best for a specific application.

Feature Extraction Methods for Text

Moving on to feature extraction, this process transforms text into quantifiable data that ML models can interpret. One traditional but powerful technique is the Term Frequency-Inverse Document Frequency (TF-IDF), which evaluates the importance of words within a document relative to a larger corpus. It highlights unique words by assigning higher weights to those that appear frequently in a document but less commonly across the dataset. N-grams take this a step further by considering combinations of words and capturing the context better than single-word analysis. Meanwhile, word embeddings, such as Word2Vec and GloVe, represent words as dense vectors in a continuous space, preserving semantic relationships. These embeddings enable models to identify similarities in meaning between words, enhancing their ability to discern nuanced categories.

When implementing feature extraction, it's helpful to consider the level of granularity needed for your task. Use TF-IDF for straightforward applications, n-grams for tasks benefitting from phrase recognition, and word embeddings when context and semantics are important.

Handling Imbalanced Datasets in Text Classification

Handling imbalanced datasets presents another challenge in text classification. Real-world data often exhibit skewed distributions, where certain classes dominate. This imbalance can lead models to favor the majority class, resulting in biased predictions. To counteract this, several strategies are employed. Oversampling the minority class or undersampling the majority class adjusts the dataset distribution to be more balanced. The Synthetic Minority Over-sampling Technique (SMOTE) generates synthetic examples for the minority class, offering a better solution without significant loss of information. Also, algorithmic approaches such as adjusting class weights or using ensemble methods, like Random Forests or Gradient Boosting, can help models learn equitably across classes.

In practice, it's advisable to experiment with multiple strategies for addressing imbalanced data. Combining oversampling with algorithmic adjustments can improve model robustness. Always validate your approach with metrics that reflect class-specific performance, such as precision, recall, and F1-score, to make sure that the classifier performs well across all categories.

Named Entity Recognition (NER)

Creating and optimizing Named Entity Recognition (NER) systems is paramount in NLP as it helps in identifying specific entities like names, dates, and locations within a text. To build effective NER systems, ML techniques are frequently employed. Among these, sequence labeling approaches such as Conditional Random Fields (CRF) have been a staple for quite some time. CRFs are advantageous because they consider the context provided by neighboring inputs, which is important in understanding the boundaries and categories of entities correctly.

Solutions for NER

However, advancements in deep learning have introduced models like Bidirectional Long Short-Term Memory with CRF (BiLSTM-CRF), which have significantly improved NER performance. These models take advantage of the BiLSTM's ability to process sequences from both directions—forward and backward—thereby offering a comprehensive view of the input data. This dual perspective allows for a better understanding of contextual relationships, leading to more accurate entity recognition. When designing NER systems using these approaches, it's important to evaluate their compatibility with your specific application needs, ensuring that you select a model that fits your complexity and computational resource requirements.

Challenges in NER for Domain-Specific Applications

One major hurdle when applying NER techniques is dealing with domain-specific texts. Standard models often struggle in these areas due to the terminology and context not typically found in general datasets. For example, medical or legal texts come with specialized vocabularies that generic NER models might misinterpret. Customization of NER systems is needed to address these sector-specific challenges. Pre-training models on domain-related corporations or implementing custom rules can help mitigate this issue, but these adjustments need careful calibration to avoid overfitting, where the model performs well on training data but poorly on unseen data.

Techniques for Improving NER Accuracy and Generalization

Several techniques are available to improve accuracy and generalization in NER models:

Transfer learning: This is one such technique where a model pre-trained on large datasets is fine-tuned with smaller, domain-specific datasets. This approach leverages existing knowledge to adapt quickly to new domains, often resulting in better performance than training a model from scratch.

Domain Adaptation: Additionally, domain adaptation strategies can be used to modify the source domain to resemble the target domain more closely, facilitating better model transferability.

Active Learning: Another method to enhance model performance is active learning, which has to do with iteratively refining models by focusing on examples most likely to yield informative insights. When selecting and annotating uncertain predictions, a system can learn efficiently and improve its accuracy incrementally.

Evaluation Metrics and Best Practices for NER Systems

Evaluating the performance of NER systems is critical to allowing them to meet the desired accuracy standards. Key metrics for assessment include precision, recall, and F1 score. Precision measures the number of correct positive results divided by all positive results predicted by the classifier, highlighting the model's exactness. Recall, or sensitivity, assesses how many relevant instances are retrieved among all relevant instances, emphasizing completeness. The F1 score balances precision and recall by calculating their harmonic mean to provide a single performance measure, which is especially useful in cases where there's an uneven class distribution.

Practical Implications of Metrics

When assessing NER systems, it is important to consider the practical implications of these metrics. High precision with low recall might indicate that while the model makes fewer errors, it also misses many entities. High recall with low precision suggests the model identifies most entities but includes many false positives. Striking a balance is crucial, depending on the context of the application, whether it prioritizes minimizing errors or capturing as many entities as possible.

Tracking these metrics over time and comparing them against benchmarks can guide continuous improvement efforts. This involves refining algorithms, updating training datasets, and recalibrating parameters to optimize the system's effectiveness.

In practice, best practices for deploying NER systems into production environments involve extensive testing, monitoring for changes in input data characteristics, and setting up feedback loops for ongoing learning. Implementation should be iterative, allowing room for tweaks based on real-world usage and end-user feedback. Robust documentation and comprehensive training for users interacting with these systems also form a cornerstone of successful deployments, making sure clarity and consistency in how NER outputs are interpreted and used.

Machine Translation

In the world of machine translation systems, a relevant element is the design and implementation of neural architectures that elevate translation quality. One prominent architecture is the sequence-to-sequence model, which uses an encoder-decoder framework to handle input and output sequences. When integrating attention mechanisms, these models can dynamically focus on different parts of input sentences when generating translations. This process mimics how humans understand language by concentrating on salient words or phrases rather than taking in entire sentences wholesale. The attention mechanism becomes particularly important when translating long and complex sentences, acting as an internal guide that improves both accuracy and coherence.

Handling Language Pairs With Limited Parallel Data

However, implementing these systems is not without challenges, especially when it comes to translating language pairs with limited parallel data. Traditional machine translation relies heavily on large datasets containing paired examples of source and target languages. In reality, such extensive parallel corpora are not always available for less common languages. To address this scarcity, researchers turn to unsupervised and semi-supervised techniques. Unsupervised learning leverages monolingual data, allowing models to learn language structure independently before attempting translation. Semi-supervised approaches, meanwhile, strategically combine limited parallel data with abundant monolingual texts, harnessing both to refine the system's understanding and output. These methods open doors for more inclusive global communication by enabling translations across underrepresented languages.

Techniques for Improving Translation Quality and Fluency

Improving translation quality doesn't stop at effective architecture or data handling techniques. Fine-tuning is critical in honing a model's effectiveness and adaptability. If adjusting pre-trained models using smaller, domain-specific datasets, developers should tailor the system to excel in particular contexts, enhancing its fluency and appropriateness. Plus, incorporating stylistic and contextual adjustments allows translations to reflect nuances such as tone, formality, or cultural references pertinent to the target language. For example, a direct translation may capture the literal meaning but fail to convey the intended emotion or implication. Through careful fine-tuning and contextual reasoning, translations can achieve a human-like touch that resonates better with users.

Deploying and Scaling Machine Translation Systems

As we consider the deployment and scalability of these machine translation systems, the conversation shifts to accommodate the demands of high-volume requests and multilingual processing. Scalability is relevant for businesses looking to offer services globally, where they must handle millions of translation queries daily. It's not merely about processing power but also infrastructure optimization.

Cloud-Based Solutions

Cloud-based solutions offer flexibility, adapting resources as demand fluctuates while maintaining cost efficiency. Beyond mere infrastructure, the intelligent orchestration of tasks allows for load balancing across servers, preventing bottlenecks and allowing swift response times.

API Interfaces

Also, deploying efficient API interfaces can streamline integration into existing applications, making machine translation services readily accessible to various platforms and user bases. Considerations extend to latency reduction, which is critical in environments requiring real-time translations, such as customer service interactions or video conferencing tools. Consistent monitoring and feedback mechanisms embedded within the system keep performance aligned with evolving user expectations, capturing insights on translation accuracy or user satisfaction to iterate improvements continually.

Ultimately, developing great machine translation systems is all about intertwining sophisticated models with strategic data utilization and thoughtful deployment planning. Each aspect complements the other, from crafting precise and flexible neural networks to innovatively managing scarce data and deploying scalable infrastructures. In working through these intricacies, software engineers go into the detail-oriented nature of machine translation—an exploration that shapes a landscape where language barriers gradually diminish, bringing the world just a little closer together.

Question Answering Systems

In the world of NLP, designing and implementing effective Question Answering (QA) systems presents both exciting opportunities and significant challenges. These systems are relevant for enabling machines to understand human language and provide meaningful responses.

Designing End-to-End QA Systems

The core of a successful QA system lies in its architecture, which often integrates both retrieval-based and generative models. Retrieval-based models focus on sifting through vast databases to extract relevant information, essentially acting as powerful search engines. Generative models, on the other hand, aim to construct responses from scratch based on learned language patterns. When combined, these models take advantage of the strengths of each approach, leading to more comprehensive and nuanced answers.

Guidelines for creating such hybrid systems involve a few key steps. Initially, defining the scope and domain of the QA system is important—this helps in curating the necessary datasets and training models appropriately. Next, it's important to develop an information retrieval layer that can efficiently filter relevant data in response to queries. Following this, a generative model can be fine-tuned on the filtered content to produce coherent answers. This dual approach increases accuracy and makes the system solid across different contexts.

Open-Domain vs. Closed-Domain QA Systems

When discussing QA systems, it is vital to differentiate between open-domain and closed-domain categories.

Open-domain systems: Such as those seen in search engines, handle a broad range of topics and need to access extensive datasets drawn from various sources. These systems thrive when abundant information is available, but they also face challenges related to filtering noise from valuable data.

Closed-domain QA systems: By contrast, focus on specialized areas where they can leverage structured and specific datasets. These systems require a profound understanding of their niche domain, which allows them to produce more precise and contextually accurate answers. While they might lack the versatility of open-domain systems, closed-domain systems excel in environments where expertise is important.

Integrating Knowledge Bases and External Information

Incorporating knowledge bases and external information is another important strategy to enhance QA systems. Knowledge bases provide structured data that can enrich a system's ability to generate precise responses. For instance, linking a QA system with a medical knowledge base enables it to provide highly detailed and reliable medical advice.

To integrate these resources effectively, developers should focus on building interfaces that facilitate seamless communication between the QA system and external databases. This process ensures compatibility in terms of data formats and establishing protocols for retrieving and processing information efficiently. The integration of such rich resources boosts the depth of answers and adds layers of validation, making sure that users receive accurate and trustworthy information.

Challenges and Solutions for Robust QA Systems

Building QA systems capable of handling diverse and complex queries comes with its own set of hurdles. One major challenge is managing the vast variability in human language, which can trip up even the most advanced models. Different phrasings, slang, and ambiguous expressions mean that QA systems must continually adapt to new linguistic inputs.

A practical solution could be using NLP techniques like synonym recognition and semantic understanding to better interpret user queries. Also, implementing ML models that learn from past interactions can help these systems evolve over time, thereby improving their ability to comprehend and respond accurately.

Scalability and performance are also critical considerations. As user demand grows, allowing the system to maintain swift response times without compromising quality becomes relevant. Techniques such as caching frequently accessed data and optimizing database queries can mitigate these issues, while cloud-based infrastructure offers scalable solutions that cater to fluctuating workloads.

Handling unexpected or out-of-scope questions needs smart fallback mechanisms. Employing strategies such as asking clarifying questions or confidently admitting uncertainty rather than providing erroneous answers can help maintain user trust while navigating these challenges.

Quizzes and Exercises

Quiz

1. What are the key differences between TF-IDF and word embeddings for feature extraction in text classification?

2. Explain the concept of imbalanced datasets in text classification. How can this issue be addressed?

3. What are the main challenges in designing Named Entity Recognition (NER) systems for domain-specific applications?

4. Compare and contrast CRF and BiLSTM-CRF approaches for Named Entity Recognition.

5. What is the encoder-decoder architecture in neural machine translation? How does it work?

Exercises

1. **Text Classification System:** Implement a text classification system for sentiment analysis using a dataset of your choice (such as movie and product reviews). Compare the performance of at least two different feature extraction methods (e.g., TF-IDF vs. word embeddings) and two different classification algorithms. Discuss the results, including how you handled any class imbalance issues.

2. **Named Entity Recognition:** Design and implement a Named Entity Recognition system for a specific domain (for example, medical texts and legal documents). Use a deep learning approach (such as BiLSTM-CRF or BERT-based model). Evaluate your system using appropriate metrics and discuss the challenges you faced in achieving good performance on domain-specific entities.

3. **Low-Resource Machine Translation:** Develop a strategy for creating a machine translation system for a language pair with limited parallel data. Outline your approach, including data collection/augmentation techniques, model architecture, and any transfer learning methods you would employ. Implement a proof-of-concept for a small subset of the languages and evaluate its performance.

Key Insights and Practical Takeaways

- **Architecture Selection:** Choose appropriate neural network architectures for specific NLP tasks. Use CNNs for capturing local text features, RNNs for understanding sequential data, and attention mechanisms for complex tasks like machine translation.

- **Data Preprocessing:** Implement thorough text preprocessing techniques, including tokenization, stemming/lemmatization, and stop-word removal, to prepare data for NLP models effectively.

- **Feature Extraction:** Utilize advanced feature extraction methods like TF-IDF, n-grams, and word embeddings to transform text into meaningful numerical representations for machine learning models.

- **Handling Challenges:** Address common NLP challenges such as imbalanced datasets in text classification, domain-specific terminology in Named Entity Recognition, and limited parallel data in machine translation using techniques like oversampling, transfer learning, and unsupervised learning approaches.

- **System Design:** Design end-to-end NLP systems that combine retrieval-based and generative models, integrate knowledge bases, and implement robust mechanisms for handling diverse queries and scaling to meet performance demands.

CHAPTER 11

Computer Vision Systems

Creating computer vision systems is like giving sight to computers, allowing them to interpret and understand the visual world around us. It's a fascinating blend of art and science, where the goal is to mimic human vision capabilities to solve real-world problems. From basic tasks like sorting images into categories to more complex ones involving video analysis, the path is about going through various challenges and employing innovative techniques. Knowing how to design these systems means going into different architectures and methods that allow computers to classify and analyze images and videos efficiently. It's about making machines capable of seeing and interpreting their surroundings with a level of precision and understanding that's essential for modern applications.

In this chapter, we will talk about the nuts and bolts of designing and implementing computer vision systems. We'll look at the significance of data in shaping these systems and how image classification lays the groundwork. We will also go over popular methodologies such as Convolutional Neural Networks (CNNs) for handling spatial features and learn about advancements like Residual Networks that tackle deeper learning challenges. Transfer learning will be introduced as a valuable approach when resources are limited, offering insights into leveraging pre-trained models for new tasks. Lastly, we'll also cover practical strategies to overcome computational constraints through distributed computing. The chapter rounds off by discussing data augmentation techniques that increase model robustness. This exploration is a primer for anyone looking to transition into ML roles or seeking to strengthen their understanding of computer vision's core components.

Image Classification

Sorting images into categories is a fundamental task in computer vision systems, driving myriad applications from facial recognition to autonomous driving. Achieving this needs well-designed techniques and architectures that can handle the diverse challenges posed by different datasets and application requirements.

Architectures for Image Classification Tasks

To begin with, understanding the choice of architecture for image classification tasks is important. Convolutional Neural Networks (CNNs) have been a staple in this domain due to their ability to automatically and adaptively learn spatial hierarchies of features through backpropagation. The layers of convolutional networks are particularly adept at capturing intricate details within an image, making them ideal for tasks ranging from simple digit recognition to complex facial identification. Also, ResNets, or Residual Networks, come into play for deeper neural networks. They address the degradation problem, where adding more layers results in worse performance, by introducing shortcut connections. These allow the model to pass information across layers without degradation, which significantly improves the depth and potency of deep learning systems in image classification.

Transfer Learning and Fine-Tuning in Image Classification

Another powerful tool in image classification is transfer learning. This technique leverages pre-trained models—originally developed for a specific task—as a starting point for a new, related task. This is especially useful when dealing with limited data resources, as it allows one to build on the general patterns recognized by the pre-trained network, fine-tuning it to suit new datasets or tasks. To give you an example, if you have a model trained on a massive image dataset like ImageNet, it already possesses a foundational understanding of various visual elements. When using transfer learning, you can adapt this model for specific niche tasks such as medical imaging or industrial inspection with minimal additional training, saving both time and computational resources.

Handling Large-Scale Image Datasets

When handling large-scale datasets, computational demands often become a bottleneck. Distributed computing emerges as an effective solution to tackle these challenges. When you spread out computational tasks across multiple nodes or clusters, distributed systems can process vast amounts of data simultaneously. This parallel processing capability speeds up the training phase, making it possible to handle datasets that otherwise would be infeasible on single-machine setups. Implementing frameworks such as Apache Hadoop or Spark can significantly streamline this process, allowing scalability while maintaining the accuracy and efficiency of the model.

Techniques for Improving Classification Accuracy and Efficiency

A key method to improve the accuracy of image classification models is data augmentation. This encompasses artificially expanding the size and diversity of your training dataset by applying various transformations to existing images, such as rotation, scaling, flipping, and color adjustments. These transformations help in creating a more generalized model because they mimic the variations an object might undergo in real-world scenarios. Data augmentation effectively increases the dataset's robustness by teaching the model to recognize objects irrespective of their orientation or lighting conditions, thus improving its predictive power.

For those transitioning to ML roles, these methodologies offer practical insights into building and refining computer vision systems. They present an opportunity to understand underlying principles while also getting hands-on experience with tools and frameworks commonly used in industry settings. For example, CNNs and ResNets are often explored through platforms like TensorFlow and PyTorch, providing intuitive interfaces to experiment and evaluate model performance.

Also, the implementation of guidelines for transfer learning and dataset management enhances one's proficiency in model optimization and deployment. It allows for systems that are theoretically sound as well as ready for real-world application, where factors such as dataset quality and system scalability are critical.

Object Detection

Today, we're getting into the fascinating world of object detection systems and their importance in identifying and classifying objects within images. This is an exciting area where cutting-edge technology meets real-world applications, from autonomous vehicles to smart cameras.

Designing Object Detection Systems

Let's start by discussing the design of systems using advanced algorithms like YOLO (You Only Look Once) and Faster R-CNN (Region-based Convolutional Neural Network). These algorithms are the backbone of many modern computer vision systems. Designing these systems is about picking the right algorithmic architecture that can accurately detect and classify objects in various scenarios. Take YOLO, for example; it's renowned for its speed and accuracy in detecting objects in a single neural network evaluation, making it particularly suitable for real-time applications. On the other hand, Faster R-CNN provides higher precision but with more computational overhead. The choice between these often depends on the specific needs of the task at hand—is speed of the essence, or is accuracy more critical?

Understanding the nuances of these algorithms is vital if you want to get ML roles. Imagine training a system capable of spotting pedestrians, traffic signs, and other vehicles in real time while driving down a busy street. This requires not just choosing the right algorithm but also fine-tuning it to meet the demands of variable environments. This leads us to the next point: optimization.

Strategies for Real-Time Object Detection

System optimization for real-time detection is a hot topic, especially in fields like autonomous driving, where split-second decisions can make all the difference. Time is of the essence, so algorithms need to be efficient. Strategies such as pruning unnecessary layers in neural networks, quantizing model weights to reduce execution time, and leveraging hardware acceleration using GPUs and TPUs have significance. A practical guideline here is to focus on reducing latency without sacrificing too much accuracy. Some might employ hybrid models that combine the speed of lightweight operations with the precision of heavier ones to strike the perfect balance.

Handling Multiple Object Classes and Varying Scales

Now, let's talk about handling multiple object classes and varying scales—quite the challenge! When you consider that objects may appear at different sizes and aspects in images, training a model to recognize them with high accuracy is no small feat. This has to do with expanding datasets to include diverse examples of each class and employing techniques like data augmentation to simulate diversity during training. Anchoring strategies in Faster R-CNN can be adapted to predict objects of different scales effectively. Implementing multi-scale feature extraction methods allows the systems to handle such variability convincingly. Visualize a security camera system that must identify both tiny insects and large vehicles—it sounds almost daunting, but with the right tools and techniques, it's entirely achievable.

Evaluation Metrics and Best Practices for Object Detection

After designing and optimizing these systems, there's a critical need to evaluate performance using appropriate metrics. While the formal inclusion of guidelines is not essential here, some best practices can increase understanding. Traditional metrics like precision, recall, and F1-score provide snapshots of performance, but for object detection, Intersection over Union (IoU) is key. It calculates how closely predicted bounding boxes overlap with the ground truth. An IoU above 0.5 is generally considered acceptable, but pushing this threshold provides extra assurance of reliability. Another useful metric is average precision (AP), which considers both precision and recall across different thresholds, thus offering a broader view of model performance. Evaluating diverse datasets that mimic real-world conditions adds another layer of credibility to your systems.

Image Generation

In the world of computer vision, one fascinating goal is the creation of realistic or artistic images using computational models. This is where generative models like GANs (Generative Adversarial Networks) and VAEs (Variational Autoencoders) come into play. These models have revolutionized the way we think about image generation, allowing us to create remarkably convincing and diverse visuals.

Generative Models for Image Synthesis

GANs, in particular, have garnered significant attention due to their structure involving two neural networks—the generator and the discriminator—competing against each other. The generator creates images while the discriminator evaluates them, distinguishing between real and synthetic images. Over time, this adversarial process refines the generator's ability to produce images that are increasingly indistinguishable from reality. This iterative learning process has opened new avenues in creative fields such as art and fashion, enabling the effortless production of imaginative content.

VAEs offer another approach by encoding images into a continuous latent space, capturing important features that define the images' characteristics. When sampling and interpolating within this space, VAEs can generate new images or variations on existing ones, providing artists and designers with a powerful tool for creativity and innovation. This ability to explore uncharted visual territories has profound implications across various domains.

Applications of Image Generation in Various Domains

Beyond the art and design, these generative models are being applied across a spectrum of industries, exemplifying their versatility. In entertainment, filmmakers use them to create lifelike CGI effects and bring fantastical worlds to life. Medical imaging also benefits greatly; synthetic data generated through these models aids in training algorithms more effectively, leading to breakthroughs in diagnostics and research. The automotive industry employs them in designing and testing self-driving cars under various simulated conditions, ensuring safety and reliability.

Challenges in Training and Deploying Generative Models

However, working with generative models has also its disadvantages. Training GANs, for example, often face issues like mode collapse—a situation where the generator produces limited varieties of outputs—and instability during the training process. Numerous strategies and improvements, such as Wasserstein GAN or spectral normalization, have been developed to tackle these problems. Researchers continue to innovate, seeking solid solutions that improve model performance and stability, paving the way for even greater advancements in this field.

Ethical Considerations in Synthetic Image Generation

Another layer of complexity arises when considering the ethical implications of synthetic images. As these models become more adept at mimicking reality, concerns about authenticity and misuse intensify. Deepfakes, which utilize GAN technology, are a prime example of the potential risks, as they can fabricate misleading videos that pose threats to privacy and trust. Addressing these ethical concerns needs a balanced approach: establishing clear guidelines and policies, promoting awareness of synthetic media's impact, and developing technologies capable of detecting and mitigating misuse.

Education and Communication in the Field

As we navigate these challenges, the role of education and communication becomes really important. Empowering engineers, scientists, and future industry leaders with knowledge about both the potential and pitfalls of generative models allows responsible deployment and innovation. In academic settings, incorporating discussions around ethics and societal impacts into curricula helps prepare students for real-world scenarios, instilling a sense of accountability in technological advancements.

Collaboration between sectors—combining the expertise of technologists, ethicists, legal professionals, and policymakers—can provide comprehensive solutions. If they pool resources and insights, stakeholders can address ethical dilemmas while harnessing the transformative power of generative models for constructive purposes. This collaborative spirit brings an environment conducive to long-term progress and societal benefit, aligning technological growth with ethical considerations.

The road towards mastering generative models for creating realistic or artistic images is both thrilling and complex. It demands a deep understanding of the intricacies involved, from the technical hurdles encountered during training to the ethical questions posed by their application. Yet, through innovation, collaboration, and conscientious practice, these challenges can be transformed into opportunities, unlocking new potential across various fields.

Video Analysis and Processing

When learning about the dynamic world of video content analysis, one of the key elements to consider is the architecture required for understanding sequences within video data. Unlike static images, videos provide temporal patterns and evolving scenes over time, necessitating sophisticated models that can decipher these changes. Exploring architectures like Recurrent Neural Networks (RNNs), Long Short-Term Memory networks (LSTMs), and Transformer-based models offers a foundation for capturing these sequential features effectively. Each of these architectures brings its own strengths; RNNs are traditionally well-suited for sequence prediction tasks, while LSTMs improve upon them by handling long-range dependencies, making them particularly useful in scenarios where capturing extended temporal patterns is key.

Architectures for Video Understanding Tasks

Consider a practical case where these architectures shine: sports analysis. In such an application, analyzing player movements or recognizing key events doesn't merely rely on spatial information from individual frames but also on the temporal flow across multiple frames. Detecting a goal being scored involves tracking the ball's movement sequence until it crosses the line, something that these temporal architectures excel at.

Techniques for Efficient Video Processing at Scale

Once a suitable architecture is chosen, efficient processing techniques become relevant to handle the vast amounts of data typically associated with video content. Videos are notorious for their size, often composed of thousands of frames per minute, which translates into enormous data volumes when processed in real time. Techniques like parallel processing, distributed computing, and using optimized libraries such as OpenCV or FFmpeg for pre-processing can alleviate some of the computational burdens. Guideline: Implementing batch-processing, caching, and employing frameworks like Apache Kafka for streaming data can significantly enhance processing efficiency, making sure that systems remain scalable and responsive, even under heavy loads.

Real-Time Video Analysis Systems

Real-time analysis systems further push these demands, requiring efficient processing and optimizations for immediate responsiveness. These systems find applications in live surveillance setups, where timely insights are critical, or in broadcasting, where any delay could disrupt viewing experiences or miss crucial moments. The design of these systems must consider latency reduction techniques and might benefit from edge computing strategies, where data processing occurs closer to the data source rather than relying solely on centralized servers. This reduces round-trip time for data transfer, thus allowing faster decision-making processes.

For instance, consider a scenario in live sports broadcasting. A real-time analysis system might need to instantly recognize and track players or identify when significant events happen—like a touchdown in

American football—so that the broadcast can switch views or overlay relevant statistics in real-time. The combination of quick data processing with great temporal pattern recognition helps in creating engaging and informative viewing experiences.

Challenges in Handling Long-Form Video Content

Finally, addressing challenges related to long-form video content is quite important, especially considering features like segmentation and summarization. Long-form videos require breaking down into meaningful segments, which aids in both analyzing and retrieving important information without manually sifting through extended footage. Automated segmentation techniques use cues from scene changes, audio signals, or content annotations to divide the video into coherent units. Summarization of algorithms helps condense lengthy content into short highlights, providing viewers or analysts with significant details minus the exhaustive watch time.

Let's take documentary filmmaking as an example. Editors can benefit immensely from automatic summarization tools that distill hours of raw footage into concise, thematic clips focused on key narrative points. ML models trained to recognize patterns and keywords pertinent to a storyline can greatly expedite this process, offering initial summaries for human editors to refine.

Quizzes and Exercises

Quiz

1. What are the key differences between CNNs and Vision Transformers for image classification tasks?

2. Explain the concept of transfer learning in the context of image classification. What are its benefits?

3. How does fine-tuning differ from training a model from scratch? When would you choose one over the other?

4. Compare and contrast YOLO and Faster R-CNN architectures for object detection.

5. What strategies can be employed to achieve real-time object detection on resource-constrained devices?

Exercises

1. **Image Classification with Transfer Learning:** Implement an image classification system using a pre-trained model on a dataset of your choice. Fine-tune the model for your specific task. Compare the performance of the fine-tuned model with a model trained from scratch on the same dataset. Discuss the results, including training time, accuracy, and generalization ability.

2. **Real-time Object Detection:** Design and implement a real-time object detection system using a lightweight architecture that can run on a mobile device or embedded system. Optimize the model for speed while maintaining acceptable accuracy. Evaluate the system's performance in terms of frames per second and mean Average Precision (mAP).

3. **GAN for Image Generation:** Implement a Generative Adversarial Network (GAN) for a specific image generation task. Train the GAN and showcase a series of generated images. Discuss the challenges you faced during training and how you addressed them. Also, consider and discuss the ethical implications of your chosen generation task.

Key Insights and Practical Takeaways

- **Architecture Selection:** Choose appropriate neural network architectures for specific computer vision tasks. Use CNNs for image classification and advanced models like YOLO or Faster R-CNN for object detection.

- **Transfer Learning:** Leverage pre-trained models and fine-tune them for specific tasks, especially when dealing with limited datasets. This approach saves time and computational resources while maintaining high performance.

- **Distributed Computing:** Implement distributed computing techniques to handle large-scale image datasets efficiently. Use frameworks like Apache Hadoop or Spark to process vast amounts of data in parallel.

- **Data Augmentation:** Employ data augmentation techniques to artificially expand and diversify training datasets, improving model robustness and generalization across various real-world scenarios.

- **Ethical Considerations:** Be aware of the ethical implications of synthetic image generation, particularly in areas like deepfakes. Develop and adhere to guidelines for responsible use of generative models.

CHAPTER 12

Recommender Systems

Recommender systems are the engines behind personalized experiences in our digital lives, from suggesting movies on streaming platforms to recommending products while shopping online. These systems have become an indispensable part of many applications, as they help users discover new content customized to their tastes and preferences. With technology advancing rapidly, understanding the intricacies behind recommender systems becomes critical for anyone looking to step into ML or data science roles. It's not all about the algorithms but also about how these systems are designed and implemented to meet the needs of different users and industries. It doesn't matter if you're a software engineer transitioning into ML or a student eager to explore deep into industry practices; getting a grasp on this topic is essential.

In this chapter, we will go into the design and implementation aspects of recommender systems, breaking down various approaches that make them tick. You'll explore collaborative filtering methods, where the focus is on leveraging existing user preferences to predict choices for others with similar tastes. We will also mention content-based filtering, where items are recommended based on their intrinsic features and similarities to what a user has previously enjoyed. But we go a little further; we'll also talk about hybrid approaches that combine the strengths of multiple models, showing how they tackle common challenges like the cold-start problem. As datasets grow increasingly large, scalability issues become significant; hence, we will look at strategies to know if recommender systems work efficiently under pressure. This path through recommender systems aims to give you practical insights and the technical grounding needed to excel in interviews and real-world applications.

Collaborative Filtering

Collaborative filtering is a popular and effective technique for building recommender systems. It's especially intriguing because it leverages the wisdom of the crowd to make personalized recommendations. The main idea is that users who have shared interests in the past will continue to do so, meaning their preferences can help predict one another's future choices. This approach is further divided into two main methodologies: user-based and item-based collaborative filtering.

User-Based vs. Item-Based Collaborative Filtering

In user-based collaborative filtering, the focus is on finding clusters of users with similar tastes or behaviors. It guesses what a given user might like based on what similar users have enjoyed. If users A and B both liked movies X and Y, and user A also liked movie Z, then there's a good chance user B might like movie Z too. This method shines when you have a lot of user behavior data but can struggle when new users enter the system, a situation known as the "cold-start problem."

On the flip side, item-based collaborative filtering looks at the relationships between items instead of users. If two items often receive similar ratings from different users, they're considered similar. This way, when a user likes an item, the system can recommend other items they haven't tried yet but are similar based on past interactions. Item-based methods tend to be more stable over time since they're less affected by constant changes in user behavior and can handle larger datasets more effectively.

Matrix Factorization Techniques for Collaborative Filtering

Matrix factorization techniques are important in improving the prediction accuracy of collaborative filtering systems. These techniques aim to simplify complex matrices of user-item interactions by breaking them down into smaller, more manageable pieces. Singular value decomposition (SVD) is one of the most well-known matrix factorization methods. It reduces the dimensionality of the data while preserving essential patterns, which helps uncover latent factors that explain observed preferences. When acknowledging these hidden dimensions, recommender systems can make more accurate predictions about user preferences.

Handling Sparsity and Scalability in Collaborative Filtering

However, one of the biggest challenges faced by collaborative filtering systems is dealing with sparsity. In large datasets, the interaction matrix is often mostly empty, with only a few entries populated for each user. Several methods can be employed to manage this sparsity and increase scalability. One approach is to use dimensionality reduction techniques, like SVD mentioned earlier, to fill in missing data. Another strategy is to employ neighborhood-based techniques that only consider a subset of relevant data, reducing computational complexity. Implementing distributed computing frameworks is also practical for scaling up operations across multiple servers, making it feasible to process massive datasets efficiently.

Evaluation Metrics for Collaborative Filtering Systems

When evaluating the effectiveness of collaborative filtering systems, it's important to have good metrics. Common evaluation metrics include precision, recall, and F1-score, which measure how well the recommendations meet user expectations. Precision focuses on the quality of recommendations by determining the proportion of relevant items out of those recommended. Recall measures the system's ability to find all relevant items within the dataset. The F1-score balances both precision and recall, giving a more comprehensive view of overall performance. Mean Absolute Error (MAE) and Root Mean Square Error (RMSE) are also used to assess prediction accuracy by comparing estimated ratings against actual user ratings.

Understanding how these systems affect user engagement and satisfaction is just as important as measuring technical precision. User feedback loops, coupled with A/B testing, can provide qualitative insights into how users interact with the system and where improvements might be needed. Also, diversity metrics should not be overlooked, as recommending a variety of items rather than sticking to safe bets can significantly enhance the user experience.

Content-Based Filtering

Content-based filtering is a staple component of recommender systems, focusing on the information or features associated with the items that need recommending and aligning them with users' observed tastes. At the heart of this approach lies feature extraction, a vital process that encompasses identifying the characteristics of items. This step is relevant because it defines how well the system can understand and represent the content in a form usable for recommendations. Feature extraction often relies on techniques like vector space models where attributes such as keywords for documents, color and shape for images, or genre and artist for music are drawn out and quantified.

Feature Extraction for Content-Based Recommendations

One key guideline when extracting features is to know that they accurately capture the item's essence without overwhelming the system with unnecessary data. To give you a quick example, in text-based systems, you might use techniques like TF-IDF (Term Frequency-Inverse Document Frequency), which helps highlight words that uniquely define documents. Another useful tactic is implementing algorithms like Word2Vec that provide word embeddings capturing semantic meanings. This tailoring allows the recommendations to align closely with user preferences, improving accuracy and relevance.

Similarity Measures in Content-Based Systems

Once features are extracted, the next step has to do with similarity measures, which help match these features to user profiles. These measures evaluate how close two sets of items or a user and an item are in terms of their features. Common approaches include Euclidean distance, cosine similarity, and Pearson correlation coefficient. Each method has its nuances. Euclidean distance works best when dealing with standardized data, while cosine similarity shines in high-dimensional spaces typical in document analysis. An intuitive example would be analyzing movie genres and matching them based on user history; by calculating similarities using cosine similarity, the system can recommend movies most aligned with a viewer's previous choices.

Combining Content-Based Filtering With Other Approaches

Integrating content-based filtering into broader recommendation strategies often leads to powerful hybrid systems that leverage the strengths of multiple approaches. When blending content-based methods with collaborative techniques, for example, systems can address some inherent limitations, such as the cold start problem, where there is insufficient data about new users or items. A good practice here is combining user profile data with collaborative filtering to fill in gaps when user-item interactions are sparse. For instance, Netflix often uses this synergy, incorporating user ratings and viewing history alongside the analysis of content features like genres and cast members to deliver fine-tuned suggestions. Guidelines for integration may involve weighing different approaches to achieve optimal performance, often through ML models that learn ideal combination strategies over time.

Pros and Cons of Content-Based Filtering with Other Approaches

Understanding the advantages and limitations of content-based recommendation systems provides additional insight into their utility and areas for improvement.

Advantages

One significant advantage is the ability to make personalized recommendations even when user interaction data is limited; by focusing solely on content, the system can consistently give suggestions as long as there are sufficient item features available. Also, these systems naturally avoid issues like the "popularity bias" innate in some collaborative systems, ensuring niche content can gain visibility.

Disadvantages

Yet, content-based filtering isn't without disadvantages. One major drawback is overspecialization, where recommendations become too narrow if the system rigidly sticks to known user preferences, failing to introduce diverse or novel content that could equally appeal to the user. Users might feel trapped in a bubble of recommendations, seeing only variations of what they've liked before. Another limitation is the setup's dependency on high-quality, well-structured features; inadequate feature representation can severely impair the effectiveness of recommendations.

To counteract this, exploring the potential of deep learning models that automatically learn complex representations of content can be beneficial. Models like convolutional neural networks (CNNs) and recurrent neural networks (RNNs) are increasingly being harnessed to derive richer feature sets, particularly in domains like image and voice recognition.

Hybrid Approaches

When it comes to recommender systems, a hybrid approach often emerges as a powerful strategy, blending multiple techniques to increase performance and user satisfaction. Essentially, designing an effective hybrid recommender system is about a deep understanding of how different elements can work together harmoniously. One must consider the algorithms in play as well as the context in which they will operate, allowing the combination to bring tangible benefits over individual methods.

When looking at the design of hybrid systems, several key components need attention.

Identify the strengths and weaknesses: You should do this for each standalone method you plan to integrate. For example, collaborative filtering excels at suggesting popular items but struggles to provide recommendations for new users or items, known as the cold-start problem.

Content-Based Methods: Conversely, content-based methods shine in suggesting new items to users based on their history but may lack diversity. Recognizing these attributes helps in configuring how these methods can complement each other effectively. Guidelines are quite relevant here: clearly define objectives, establish evaluation metrics, and make sure data availability aligns with your goals.

Techniques for Combining Multiple Recommendation Strategies

Techniques for combining recommendation approaches are very important to optimizing a hybrid system's performance.

Weighted Hybrid Model

One common strategy is the weighted hybrid model, where different recommendation sources are assigned specific weights reflecting their perceived accuracy or importance. In practice, this needs an iterative process of tuning these weights based on feedback and performance analytics.

Switching Hybrids

Another popular technique is switching hybrids, where the system decides, often based on certain heuristics or thresholds, which algorithm to use at any given time. This method provides flexibility by adapting to changing user needs or data characteristics without manual intervention.

Feature Augmentation Strategies

There are also feature augmentation strategies where outputs from one recommendation engine become inputs for another. This layering of information can create a better user experience by capturing a broader range of user preferences and behaviors. To implement these techniques successfully, it's crucial to maintain a solid testing framework since experimentation is key to finding the right balance and configuration of algorithms. A structured set of guidelines on choosing and refining these methods allows scalability and adaptability as user bases grow and evolve.

Adaptive Hybrid Systems that Adjust to User Behavior

Moving beyond static designs, adaptive hybrid systems come into play by automatically adjusting to evolving user behavior. These systems leverage real-time data processing and ML models to refine their recommendations continuously. Consider a streaming service that tracks user interactions with media content as well as with the platform itself—such as skipping songs or rewinding parts of a movie. When incorporating these interactions, the system learns to predict and adjust the recommendations more accurately over time, thus enhancing user engagement and satisfaction.

Adaptive systems often employ reinforcement learning, a branch of AI where agents learn optimal behaviors through trial and error. This method allows the recommender to improve its predictions by receiving feedback on which recommendations were successful. Integrating reinforcement learning within a hybrid system can give significant value, particularly in rapidly changing environments where traditional batch training might fall short. The key is creating an infrastructure that supports constant updates and learning cycles without overwhelming computational resources. While implementing adaptive solutions, developers should focus on flexibility, enabling swift iterations to keep up with dynamic user behaviors and preferences.

Case Studies of Successful Hybrid Recommender Systems

Finally, examining case studies of successful hybrid recommender systems offers valuable insights into practical implementations. Take Netflix as an example, known for its sophisticated recommendation algorithms. They employ a hybrid approach that combines collaborative filtering with content-based and personalized ranking algorithms to deliver engaging and diverse content to viewers (Krysik, 2024). Their model notably integrates user viewing history with metadata about each film or show, resulting in highly customized suggestions. Analyzing such examples highlights the importance of having a well-defined strategy for integrating multiple recommendation techniques while continuously evaluating their effectiveness.

Another notable case study comes from Amazon, which has long been a pioneer in using recommender systems to drive sales. Amazon uses item-to-item collaborative filtering, which looks at similarities between products rather than users (Hardesty, 2019). Coupled with hybrid techniques that incorporate browsing history and purchase patterns, their system provides accurate and timely product suggestions. If you study these successful implementations, you can gain a deeper appreciation for hybrid systems' role in driving business outcomes and improving user experiences.

Real-Time and Context-Aware Recommendations

Real-time recommendation systems are transforming how users interact with digital platforms, turning the experience more dynamic and personalized. The key thing about these systems is that they are great architectural frameworks that enable the swift processing of data to deliver instantaneous suggestions. To build an efficient real-time recommendation system, it's important to design architectures that can handle high volumes of data rapidly. This encompasses leveraging technologies like Apache Kafka for real-time data streaming and frameworks such as Apache Flink or Spark Streaming to process data in motion. These tools allow the system to collect, analyze, and act on information almost instantly.

Architectures for Real-Time Recommendation Systems

A central aspect of building these systems is making sure there's scalability. As user bases grow, the architecture must support increasing demands without latency issues. Microservices architectures are particularly effective here, as they allow different components of the recommendation engine to scale independently. This modular approach also facilitates easy updates and maintenance, important when personalizing recommendations at speed.

Incorporating Contextual Information in Recommendations

Contextual information has an important role in improving the relevance of real-time recommendations. Unlike traditional methods, context-aware systems consider factors like time, location, device type, and even weather conditions when making suggestions. Say, for instance, a music app might recommend upbeat tracks on a sunny morning but switch to calming melodies during late-night hours. When integrating contextual cues, these systems become adaptive to individual user situations, resulting in more pertinent and satisfying recommendations.

Implementing context-aware recommendations requires a keen understanding of how to gather and interpret contextual data. Sensor inputs from smartphones, GPS data, and historical usage patterns are valuable sources. However, designers must also understand user privacy and adhere to ethical guidelines while handling sensitive information. ML models trained to detect and respond to contextual triggers are key to transforming raw data into actionable insights.

Handling Cold-Start Problems in Real-Time Scenarios

One significant hurdle in real-time recommendation systems is the cold-start problem, which occurs when there isn't enough data about a new user or item to make informed recommendations. Addressing this challenge needs a mix of innovative strategies.

Content-Based Filtering: One approach is using content-based filtering initially to suggest items based on characteristics similar to those of items a user has shown interest in previously. Additionally, hybrid models that combine collaborative filtering techniques with other methods can help use available data more effectively. These approaches ensure that even new users receive relevant recommendations without delay.

Exploration Tactics and Personalization: Another strategy is employing exploration tactics alongside personalization. This helps in overcoming the cold start and broadens the spectrum of recommendations delivered to users. A/B testing and multi-armed bandit algorithms are often used to decide when to explore new items and when to exploit known preferences. This balance between exploration and exploitation helps create a rich user experience by introducing users to diverse possibilities they might not encounter otherwise.

Balancing Personalization and Exploration in Recommendations

Discussing the balance between personalization and exploration highlights the importance of diversifying content to keep users engaged. While excessive personalization can lead to a "filter bubble" effect where users are only exposed to familiar ideas, incorporating diverse elements prevents monotony and promotes discovery. Implementing diversity can be achieved through techniques like result diversification, which intentionally injects varied content into recommendation lists. This practice allows users to get a well-rounded experience, potentially discovering interests they weren't aware of before.

Plus, balancing these elements involves continuously monitoring and analyzing user interactions to refine the system's response. Feedback loops, aided by ML algorithms, adapt recommendations based on user behavior over time. Regular evaluations of recommendation efficiency and user satisfaction metrics are critical in adjusting strategies to optimize both personalization and exploration.

Real-time and context-aware recommendation systems present exciting opportunities and challenges in equal measure. Understanding the architectural foundations necessary for their development lays the groundwork for efficient performance. When adding contextual data, developers can craft better recommendations that resonate more deeply with users' immediate needs and circumstances. Techniques to mitigate cold-start problems allow newcomers to be as engaged as seasoned users.

Quizzes and Exercises

Quiz

1. What are the key differences between user-based and item-based collaborative filtering?

2. Explain the concept of matrix factorization in collaborative filtering. How does it address the sparsity problem?

3. What are some common evaluation metrics for recommender systems? How do they differ from traditional classification metrics?

4. In content-based filtering, what types of features are typically used for different domains (like movies, articles, and products)?

5. How do hybrid recommender systems combine collaborative and content-based approaches? Give an example.

Exercises

1. **Collaborative Filtering Implementation:** Implement a collaborative filtering recommender system using both user-based and item-based approaches. Use a dataset of your choice (such as MovieLens, or Last.fm dataset). Compare the performance of both approaches using appropriate evaluation metrics. Discuss the scalability challenges you encountered and how you addressed them.

2. **Content-Based Recommender:** Develop a content-based recommender system for a specific domain (like news articles, or job postings). Implement feature extraction techniques suitable for your chosen domain. Evaluate the system's performance and discuss the pros and cons of your approach compared to collaborative filtering.

3. **Hybrid Recommender System:** Design and implement a hybrid recommender system that combines collaborative filtering and content-based approaches. Use a real-world dataset and demonstrate how your hybrid approach overcomes the limitations of individual methods. Evaluate the system's performance and discuss any trade-offs made in your design.

Key Insights and Practical Takeaways

- **Content-Based Filtering:** Extract relevant features from items using techniques like TF-IDF or Word2Vec. Employ similarity measures such as cosine similarity to match item features with user preferences, enabling personalized recommendations even with limited user data.

- **Hybrid Approaches:** Combine multiple recommendation strategies to overcome individual limitations. Use techniques like weighted models, switching hybrids, or feature augmentation to create more robust and accurate recommender systems.

- **Real-Time and Context-Aware Systems:** Design scalable architectures using technologies like Apache Kafka and Spark Streaming for instant recommendations. Incorporate contextual information (e.g., time, location, etc.) to enhance relevance and adapt to user situations.

- **Personalization vs. Exploration:** Balance tailored recommendations with diverse content to prevent filter bubbles. Implement exploration tactics like A/B testing and multi-armed bandit algorithms to introduce users to new items while maintaining personalization.

CHAPTER 13

Time Series and Anomaly Detection

Time series analysis and anomaly detection are essential techniques in the world of predictive modeling. Regardless of predicting sales trends or spotting suspicious activity, knowing these concepts can lead to impactful insights. The key factor lies in how data behaves over time and being able to identify the unexpected when it happens. This chapter explores designing systems that can handle time series data efficiently while keeping an eye out for those anomalies that could signal something significant. Once you know these skills, you get to unravel patterns and behaviors in data that might otherwise remain hidden, turning your analytical road both exciting and rewarding.

In this chapter, you'll find a thorough exploration of forecasting models like ARIMA, Prophet, and LSTM, each bringing its own strengths to the table depending on the data's characteristics. Knowing how and when to apply these models will be invaluable for anyone who wants to predict future trends with confidence. We will also explore strategies for real-time anomaly detection, illustrating how to set up systems that alert you the moment something unexpected occurs. Dealing with concept drift is another key focus, as adjusting to changing data can make all the difference in maintaining model accuracy over time. We'll also mention seasonal adjustment techniques that help bring clarity to datasets filled with periodic fluctuations. So gear up to add some powerful analytical tools to your repertoire, perfect for tackling real-world challenges and impressing your audience during tech interviews.

Forecasting Models

Time series forecasting is a critical aspect of ML, especially when dealing with data that spans over time. The primary goal here is to understand how various models can help predict future values based on historical data. This encompasses several techniques, each with its own strengths and applications.

Time Series Forecasting Techniques

ARIMA

Let's start with ARIMA (AutoRegressive Integrated Moving Average), a classical method in time series forecasting. ARIMA is particularly effective when the data exhibits a linear trend over time and when seasonality needs careful consideration but isn't overpowering. This works well for datasets with quarterly sales figures or yearly temperature recordings. The model is composed of three parts: autoregressive terms, differencing steps to make the data stationary, and moving average components. When tuning these components, ARIMA can be customized to fit a wide range of time series data effectively.

Prophet

Another popular tool is Prophet, developed by Facebook. It's designed to handle missing data points and outliers while accommodating holidays and seasonality with ease. Prophet is known for its flexibility and user-friendly nature, making it a great choice for those new to time series forecasting. Think of scenarios like predicting website traffic where weekly patterns are evident but fluctuating considerably during certain events; Prophet efficiently manages such fluctuations by adjusting seasonality parameters.

LSTM

Then there's LSTM, or Long Short-Term Memory networks, which belong to the family of recurrent neural networks (RNNs). LSTMs are particularly well-suited for complex time series that have long-range dependencies. They shine in scenarios where you need to capture intricate temporal patterns, a task often challenging for traditional methods. An example might be predicting stock market trends, where past information significantly impacts future movements, and hidden layers in LSTM models can capture these dependencies more effectively than simpler approaches.

Handling Seasonality and Trends in Time Series Data

While understanding individual models is quite relevant here, accounting for seasonality and trends in time series can lead to more accurate forecasts. Seasonality has to do with periodic fluctuations, like higher retail sales during holidays, whereas trends indicate long-term movements, such as a gradual increase in temperature due to climate change. Ignoring these aspects can skew forecasts, leading to inaccurate predictions. Proper handling allows the model to capture the essence of the data's behavior over time.

Multivariate Time Series Forecasting Approaches

Multivariate forecasting is essential when dealing with multiple interrelated variables. Say you're trying to predict electricity demand: This is influenced by factors like temperature, time of day, and even significant sporting events. Multivariate models consider these interconnected variables together, offering a comprehensive view. This approach improves accuracy but uncovers relationships between different factors that might go unnoticed in univariate analysis.

Evaluating and Comparing Different Forecasting Models

Evaluating and comparing forecasting models is another key part of the process. It's about choosing one technique and about determining which method suits your specific dataset best. Techniques like cross-validation and backtesting can help measure the predictive performance of different models. Once you compare metrics such as mean squared error (MSE) or mean absolute error (MAE), you can identify models that provide the most reliable forecasts. This step is important because a model that performs exceptionally well on one dataset might not fare as well on another with different characteristics.

For software engineers transitioning into ML roles or data scientists preparing for technical interviews, acknowledging these concepts adds practical value. These professionals must consider the theoretical underpinnings of each model and real-world implementation challenges too. For instance, handling large volumes of time-stamped data or managing high-dimensional datasets needs both knowledge and experience with system design principles.

In this context, guidelines are a roadmap to success. When working with ARIMA, make sure the data is stationary; otherwise, the model may produce misleading results. With Prophet, incorporate domain-specific holidays to improve accuracy, and when using LSTM, pay attention to hyperparameter tuning, as it can greatly affect the model's effectiveness.

Real-Time Anomaly Detection

When it comes to building real-time anomaly detection systems, having a clear understanding of the building blocks is quite crucial. Think about it—in an ever-changing data environment, where streams of information constantly flow in and out, detecting anomalies as soon as they happen is key. Real-time architectures make this possible by continuously processing data and immediately flagging anything abnormal. Just picture a system that acts like a vigilant guard, keeping watch over your data and raising alarms the moment something seems off. This immediate detection capability is vital for applications like fraud detection in financial services or monitoring critical infrastructure for faults.

Statistical vs. ML Approaches to Anomaly Detection

Now, let's have a look at how these systems work:

Statistical Methods

Statistical methods offer one approach, relying on mathematical principles to spot deviations from what's considered "normal." It's like following a blueprint that outlines expected behavior; any deviation suggests an anomaly. Calculating the mean and standard deviation of a dataset can help identify values that fall outside the normal range. However, while effective, statistical methods might not always capture more complex anomalies.

ML Approaches

That's where ML comes in. Unlike statistical approaches, ML relies on algorithms designed to learn patterns from data and discern unusual activities. These models are trained on historical data to recognize what typical behavior looks like and subsequently detect irregularities. For example, clustering techniques like K-means can group similar data points, allowing anything that doesn't fit well within a cluster to stand out as an anomaly. You can think of it as teaching a system to understand what normalcy looks like and then pointing out anything that raises an eyebrow.

Handling High-Dimensional Data in Anomaly Detection

But it's not all smooth sailing. High-dimensional data has its own challenges in anomaly detection. When you're dealing with datasets that have many features, the complexity increases exponentially. Imagine if you're trying to find a needle in a haystack where the haystack has multiple layers and dimensions. This needs sophisticated techniques to accurately pinpoint outliers without getting overwhelmed by the sheer volume of information. Advanced methods, such as dimensionality reduction techniques like Principal Component Analysis (PCA), can help simplify the data while preserving the key characteristics needed for effective anomaly detection.

Balancing Precision and Recall in Anomaly Detection Systems

With all this technology, balancing precision and recall becomes another essential aspect.

Precision: Precision refers to the accuracy of the anomaly detection system—its ability to correctly identify true anomalies without mistaking normal behavior as anomalous.

Recall: This measures the completeness of the system—how well it captures all actual anomalies. Striking the right balance between precision and recall is very important. A model too focused on precision might miss genuine anomalies, while one that emphasizes recall could flood you with false alarms. This balance allows for the anomaly detection systems to be both efficient and reliable.

For engineers venturing into ML roles, knowing about these components isn't just about building a system; it's about crafting solutions that are resilient, adaptable, and scalable. Nowadays, with tech interviews, articulating your thought process behind designing such systems can set you apart. Drawing from real-world scenarios can be particularly influential here. Consider a streaming service predicting customer churn by pinpointing unusual user behaviors that signal dissatisfaction or intent to leave. An engineer who comprehends how to integrate real-time architectures, leverage statistical and ML methodologies, tackle high-dimensional data, and maintain a balance between precision and recall will be well-equipped to design great anomaly detection solutions.

And for graduates who want to enter the field, grasping these key principles lays a solid foundation upon which to build expertise. Going into hands-on projects or case studies involving anomaly detection can provide invaluable insights into the practical challenges and solutions associated with real-time systems. It's about building confidence and competence in translating theoretical concepts into tangible, working models.

Handling Concept Drift

Within the time series analysis, one cannot overlook the formidable challenge of concept drift. This phenomenon reflects changes in the statistical properties of the data over time, which in turn can lead to a degradation in model performance if not properly managed. Identifying these shifts is crucial to maintaining the accuracy and reliability of predictions, as they signify that the underlying data distributions are evolving. Think of it like this: when you're driving on a familiar road, but suddenly there's unexpected construction; you need to adapt your route to continue safely. In the same way, recognizing concept drift allows systems to recalibrate effectively.

Detecting and Adapting to Concept Drift in Time Series Data

To address concept drift, we first need to detect it accurately. One effective technique is about setting up monitoring mechanisms for identifying deviations that might indicate such drifts. To give you an example, statistical tests and control charts can help pinpoint anomalies in data trends over time, serving as early warning systems. Developing intuition about when concept drift is occurring—and identifying its potential impact on models—ensures that predictive accuracy doesn't take a hit.

Online Learning Algorithms for Dynamic Environments

Once concept drift is identified, adaptability becomes quite relevant. Online learning algorithms are indispensable tools in this scenario. These algorithms are designed to continuously update themselves, incorporating new data to reflect shifting characteristics in dynamic environments. Unlike traditional batch learning methods that require retraining models from scratch, online learning facilitates seamless updates without disrupting ongoing operations. It's similar to updating software applications on your device, making sure they remain functional and efficient as new features or security patches become available.

Techniques for Model Retraining and Updating in Production

Regular retraining and model updates are also important in managing concept drift. To keep performance levels consistent, it's important to establish a routine schedule for updating models based on fresh data inputs. Picture athletes needing constant training to remain at peak performance; similarly, ML models require continual tuning to stay relevant. The process can involve several strategies, including retraining with recent data batches or employing ensemble methods to combine insights from multiple models for a more robust approach.

When tackling concept drift, another critical aspect is all about evaluating the effectiveness of deployed solutions. Monitoring model performance under drift conditions allows us to assess their resilience and adaptability. Establishing comprehensive evaluation metrics provides a clear picture of how well models are responding to the changes. When examining indicators such as prediction error rates, accuracy scores, or other relevant measurements, teams can gauge whether interventions are successful or if further adjustments are necessary.

Evaluating Model Performance Under Concept Drift

Guidelines for implementing these evaluations can help streamline processes and ensure consistency. For instance, defining acceptable thresholds for error margins can give teams a benchmark against which they measure success. Also, integrating regular performance checks into the workflow allows for proactive responses to any detected shifts, avoiding potential pitfalls down the line.

Practical examples highlight the importance of these concepts in real-world scenarios. Consider an e-commerce platform experiencing varying user behavior patterns due to seasonal sales events or external economic factors—concept drift here could mean changing customer preferences that affect recommendation systems. Once continuous learning techniques and periodic updates are applied, the platform can better anticipate demand fluctuations and adjust recommendations accordingly, increasing user satisfaction and business outcomes.

Lastly, promoting a culture of awareness around concept drift within teams is beneficial. Encouraging collaboration among data scientists, engineers, and stakeholders promotes a shared understanding of this challenge, allowing for more informed decision-making and problem-solving. Regular workshops or knowledge-sharing sessions focused on tackling concept drift can improve the collective capability to handle evolving data landscapes adeptly.

Seasonal Adjustment Techniques

Going on this path of time series analysis can be an enlightening experience, especially with seasonal adjustment techniques. These techniques let data scientists and engineers slice through the noise and uncover underlying trends and patterns. To start with, let's talk about decomposing a time series into its fundamental components: trend, seasonality, and residuals.

Methods for Decomposing Time Series

Say you're looking at sales data over several years. At first glance, this data may seem chaotic and unpredictable due to various influencing factors. However, if you decompose it, you'll notice a trend component indicating a long-term movement, either upward or downward. Then there's the seasonal component, which reveals recurring patterns that might happen weekly, monthly, or annually. The residuals are what's left after removing the trend and seasonality—essentially the random noise or irregular effects. Decomposing data in this way is like peeling layers from an onion; each layer brings you closer to knowing the main behavior of your dataset. And this understanding is really important when developing accurate forecasting models.

Seasonal Adjustment in Forecasting Models

But things start happening when you apply seasonal adjustments to these decomposed components, particularly targeting the seasonality. Once you strip away periodic fluctuations, you're left with a deseasonalized version of the data. This process clarifies the long-term trend and residual variance, making it significantly easier to predict future movements. Imagine trying to forecast tourist visits to a beach resort. When adjusting for summer peaks and winter lows, you obtain a cleaner dataset that reflects true growth or decline, independent of predictable seasonal ups and downs. This refined dataset improves the accuracy of forecasting models, leading to smarter, data-driven decisions.

Handling Multiple Seasonal Patterns in Time Series Data

Remember the importance of managing multiple seasonal patterns. In reality, datasets often contain more than one cyclical pattern. For example, electricity usage can exhibit daily and yearly cycles—more power is used during the day than at night, and usage spikes in winter months. Failing to account for these overlapping cycles may skew predictions and lead to inaccuracies. Therefore, handling multiple seasonal patterns becomes critical in obtaining reliable forecasts. Techniques such as Fourier analysis or advanced algorithms like TBATS (Trigonometric, Box-Cox transformation, ARIMA errors, Trend and Seasonal components) allow you to model these complex structures effectively.

Impact on Seasonal Adjustment on Anomaly Detection

Seasonal adjustment makes forecasting better, but it is just as important in anomaly detection. When anomalies are identified, they need to represent genuine deviations from expected behavior rather than normal seasonal variability. Think about monitoring internet traffic for a popular website. Regular ups and downs might reflect nightly drops in visitors, while an actual anomaly could indicate a sudden loss in traffic due to a server issue. When you apply seasonal adjustments, you strip away these regular variations, making sure that what remains stands out as truly unusual. This approach improves the reliability of detecting real anomalies, enhancing system response and troubleshooting efficiency.

Ultimately, implementing seasonal adjustment techniques provides software engineers, aspiring ML professionals, and seasoned data scientists with a toolkit for gaining deeper insights into time series data. More importantly, these insights align directly with the types of challenges faced in technical interviews and real-world applications. It doesn't matter if you're aiming to refine forecasts or sharpen anomaly detection systems; mastering seasonal adjustment techniques is a relevant skill, offering clarity in areas where confusion once reigned.

Remember that when decomposing time series data, it's helpful to choose appropriate methods like additive or multiplicative decomposition based on the nature of the dataset. Additive decomposition works well when seasonal variation is relatively constant, whereas multiplicative decomposition suits situations where seasonal patterns increase or decrease proportionally to the level of the series.

Quizzes and Exercises

Quiz

1. Compare and contrast ARIMA and LSTM models for time series forecasting. In what scenarios would you prefer one over the other?

2. What is the purpose of seasonal decomposition in time series analysis?

3. Explain the concept of stationarity in time series data. Why is it important for certain forecasting models?

4. How does multivariate time series forecasting differ from univariate forecasting? Give an example of when you might use each.

5. What are the main differences between statistical and machine learning approaches to anomaly detection?

Exercises

1. **Time Series Forecasting Comparison:** Implement three different time series forecasting models (e.g., ARIMA, Prophet, and LSTM) on a publicly available dataset (such as stock prices or weather data). Compare their performance using appropriate metrics (e.g., RMSE, MAE, MAPE). Discuss the strengths and weaknesses of each model in the context of your chosen dataset.

2. **Real-time Anomaly Detection System:** Design and implement a real-time anomaly detection system for a streaming data scenario (like server metrics, IoT sensor data). Your system should be able to process incoming data points and flag anomalies in near real-time. Implement both a statistical approach (e.g., moving average with standard deviation) and a ML approach (e.g., Isolation Forest or LOF). Compare their performance in terms of accuracy and computational efficiency.

3. **Handling Concept Drift:** Develop a system that can detect and adapt to concept drift in a time series dataset. Use a dataset where concept drift is likely to occur (such as retail sales data spanning several years, including periods of economic changes). Implement an online learning algorithm that can update the model as new data arrives. Evaluate your system's ability to maintain performance over time compared to a static model.

Key Insights and Practical Takeaways

- **Forecasting Models:** Implement ARIMA for linear trends, Prophet for handling seasonality and missing data, and LSTM for complex time series with long-range dependencies. Consider multivariate approaches when dealing with interrelated variables to improve prediction accuracy.

- **Real-Time Anomaly Detection:** Design scalable architectures that process data streams continuously. Combine statistical methods and ML approaches like clustering to identify anomalies effectively. Balance precision and recall to minimize false alarms while capturing genuine anomalies.

- **Concept Drift Management:** Implement monitoring mechanisms to detect changes in data distributions over time. Utilize online learning algorithms for continuous model updates, and establish regular retraining schedules to maintain model accuracy in dynamic environments.

- **Seasonal Adjustment Techniques:** Decompose time series into trend, seasonality, and residual components. Apply seasonal adjustments to reveal underlying trends and improve forecasting accuracy. Handle multiple seasonal patterns using advanced techniques like Fourier analysis or TBATS for complex cyclical data.

- **Performance Evaluation:** Regularly assess model performance under concept drift conditions. Establish comprehensive evaluation metrics and acceptable thresholds for error margins. Foster a culture of awareness around evolving data landscapes within teams to promote informed decision-making.

CHAPTER 14

Reinforcement Learning Systems

Reinforcement learning (RL) systems are transforming the way we deal with complex problems in various industries. These systems, which once thrived only in academic circles and theoretical constructs, have made their way into real-world production and multi-agent environments. As we get to know more about RL, you'll find out how these advanced systems can be designed and implemented to handle demanding tasks. Whether optimizing logistics or managing financial trades, RL systems are reshaping the industry by introducing innovative solutions that adapt to evolving challenges. In this chapter, we lift the hood on RL systems, revealing their inner workings and potential in modern applications.

Here, we will understand the design and implementation of RL systems, particularly focusing on production environments and scenarios where multiple agents come into play. We'll mention relevant aspects of architecting RL systems that blend seamlessly with existing infrastructure. This allows for efficient operation without disrupting current workflows. You'll also learn about the hurdles faced when applying RL algorithms outside the controlled lab setting, including handling unpredictability and the need for systems to adjust quickly to new data. We'll talk about the strategic considerations of balancing exploration and exploitation to improve decision-making while maintaining stability. Safety protocols and ethical guidelines will also be discussed, highlighting practices relevant to deploying RL systems in critical areas like healthcare and autonomous driving. Finally, we'll venture into the multi-agent systems, examining how coordinated agent interactions can lead to superior outcomes and how scalability challenges can be managed effectively. So, prepare to uncover intriguing insights into the design and deployment of RL systems that could redefine the future of technology.

RL in Production

RL has come a long way from theoretical models to being deployed in practical applications across industries. Knowing how to integrate RL models into existing systems is important for ensuring they operate seamlessly and efficiently in real-world settings.

Challenges in Applying RL to Real-World Problems

There are a few challenges to consider when it comes to applying RL to real-world problems.

Architecture Design

One of the primary challenges in deploying RL models is related to architecture design. The architecture must be able to support the integration of the RL model without disrupting the workflow of existing systems. For example, consider a logistics company looking to optimize delivery routes using RL. The company must design an architecture that allows the RL model to interact with current routing databases and software, updating paths in real time as new data comes in. An effective RL system architecture should facilitate communication between various components, leveraging APIs or middleware solutions where necessary to maintain seamless operation.

Variability and Unpredictability

In addition to architecture design, applying RL algorithms to solve real-world problems comes with its own set of difficulties. One such challenge is the variability and unpredictability of real-world environments compared to controlled simulations. The market demands can change rapidly, requiring RL models to adapt on the fly. An example is the use of RL in finance, where models must quickly adjust to fluctuations in stock prices and market trends to make profitable decisions. This needs careful consideration of how RL algorithms are trained and updated, making sure continuous learning and adaptation capabilities are in place.

Handling Exploration vs. Exploitation in Production Systems

Balancing exploration and exploitation is another key aspect when deploying RL in production environments. In simple terms, exploration encompasses trying new actions to discover their effects, while exploitation leverages known information to maximize reward. Striking a balance is important to optimize decision-making processes without compromising system stability. Consider an online recommendation system that uses RL to suggest products to users. Too much exploration might result in irrelevant recommendations, leading users to abandon the site. On the flip side, excessive exploitation could cause the system to miss out on introducing new, potentially successful items. To manage this, techniques like epsilon-greedy strategies or softmax action selection can be employed, allowing the system to optimize its approach over time.

Safety Considerations in RL-Based Decision-Making Systems

Safety is important in systems relying on automated decision-making, particularly in critical applications such as healthcare or autonomous vehicles. Implementing safety protocols and guidelines is relevant to mitigate risks associated with RL-based decision-making. To give you a quick example, self-driving cars using RL models must adhere to strict safety standards to allow passengers and pedestrians to remain unharmed. This involves creating fail-safes and redundant systems to override RL decisions when needed or adding constraints to the model's learning process to prevent unsafe actions.

Guidelines for ensuring safety in RL systems often include defining "safe" action spaces, monitoring outputs to detect anomalies, and instituting human oversight mechanisms. In fields like healthcare, where RL may be used to recommend treatment plans, regulatory compliance checks can be used as additional layers of security. Testing models extensively in simulated environments before real-world deployment helps identify and rectify potential issues, and so, reaching smoother transitions to practical use.

Multi-Agent Systems

When getting into multi-agent environments within RL, one of the first considerations is designing simulated settings where numerous agents can interact, learn, and evolve collaboratively. Essentially, RL is all about training algorithms to make optimal decisions by interacting with their environment. When multiple agents are introduced, these interactions become more complex but also more representative of real-world scenarios. For example, consider a traffic management system where autonomous vehicles must operate efficiently without human oversight. When creating simulated environments, we can replicate this complexity, allowing each agent—representing a vehicle—to learn from both its surroundings and the actions of other agents.

Designing Multi-Agent Reinforcement Learning Environments

One effective guideline for designing these multi-agent environments is to make sure they mirror real-world dynamics as closely as possible. Incorporating stochastic elements, like unexpected weather changes or random traffic incidents, increases the fidelity of the simulation. The goal is to create a space where agents can experiment safely, developing strategies that may later be transferred to real-world applications. Also, this method allows researchers to identify potential bottlenecks or inefficiencies in early stages, facilitating iterative improvement.

Coordination and Competition in Multi-Agent RL

Once a simulation environment is established, understanding how agents coordinate and compete becomes absolutely essential.

Coordination: This might involve agents working together to achieve a common goal, such as drones collaborating to optimize delivery routes.

Competition: However, competition could arise in resource-limited scenarios where agents vie for dominance, like trading bots aiming for maximum profit.

These dynamics need sophisticated algorithms capable of decision-making and also predicting and adapting to the behaviors of others.

Coordination among agents can lead to enhanced cooperation, producing results greater than the sum of their parts. Just picture for a second a fleet of rescue robots searching for survivors after a natural disaster. When properly coordinated, they can cover vast areas efficiently, ensuring no zone is overlooked. Conversely, in competitive settings, strategic rivalry can drive innovation and sharpen decision-making processes. A classic example comes from gaming environments; think about AI opponents in multiplayer strategy games that continually adapt their tactics based on player moves.

Scalability Challenges in Multi-Agent Systems

The benefit of incorporating multiple agents comes with unique scalability challenges. As more agents are introduced, the complexity increases exponentially, presenting hurdles in computation and communication. Each additional agent adds layers of interaction dynamics to account for, complicating the learning model significantly. To manage this effectively, engineers often employ parallel processing techniques and distributed computing strategies. This way, they can tackle large-scale problems faster and more efficiently. It's essential to balance scalability without sacrificing performance, focusing on optimizing algorithms to handle increased demands.

Applications of Multi-Agent RL in Complex Environments

Evaluating the effectiveness of multi-agent RL in practical applications reveals its transformative potential. Consider autonomous driving—a field requiring seamless navigation through dynamic, unpredictable environments. Here, RL systems need to manage self-driving cars and pedestrians, cyclists, and traditional vehicles, all while adjusting to legal and environmental constraints. In simulated environments, RL agents are trained relentlessly, refining their decision-making skills until they can navigate real-world streets with minimal supervision.

Resource management provides another intriguing use case. Think of power grids where demand fluctuates rapidly. Multi-agent RL models can predict consumption patterns, dynamically allocating resources to prevent outages and reduce waste. This kind of application showcases RL's ability to adaptively respond to varying conditions, allowing decisions that optimize operational efficiency.

Challenges and Considerations

Improving sample efficiency is a fundamental task in RL. The aim here is to maximize the use of training data without drowning in computational overload. Say you're teaching a child to ride a bike; if you could help them learn with fewer attempts, you'd save both energy and time. Similarly, in RL, promoting sample efficiency means the agent learns effectively from limited experiences. This challenge requires smart strategies like implementing advanced algorithms that make better use of available data. Techniques such as transfer learning, which allows leveraging previous knowledge for new tasks, are valuable here. If an agent knows how to navigate one type of terrain, it can generalize those skills to somewhat similar terrains, minimizing the necessity for extensive retraining.

Dealing With Partial Observability and Uncertainty

Partial observability and uncertainty often resemble trying to win a game while blindfolded. In many real-world scenarios, the complete state of the environment isn't fully visible to the agent, turning decision-making tricky. To tackle this, RL engineers need models that anticipate hidden states and accurately infer missing information. Using methods beyond standard Markov Decision Processes (MDPs), such as Partially Observable MDPs (POMDPs), helps agents make informed decisions even with limited visibility. These models consider actions taken based on belief states—essentially educated guesses about the current situation. Take autonomous driving vehicles, for example; they frequently deal with uncertain elements like unpredictable pedestrian behavior or sudden weather changes, yet must still maintain effective operations by continually updating their 'belief' of the road conditions.

Reward Shaping and Curriculum Learning Techniques

Reward shaping and curriculum learning act as guiding lights within the murky waters of RL. Reward shaping modifies the reward signal to accelerate learning, providing intermediate rewards for achieving smaller milestones. Think of it as giving a dog treats when they roll over as well as for every successful step toward rolling over. Curriculum learning, meanwhile, introduces tasks in an order that follows increasing complexity, much like a well-structured school curriculum. You can start with simpler challenges and gradually introduce more difficult ones. That way, you can build their capabilities systematically. It's important to deal with this process thoughtfully—improper structuring can mislead the agent's learning path, much like giving toddlers algebra before arithmetic.

Ethical Considerations in RL System Design

When deploying RL systems, ethical considerations must take center stage. The integration of RL in real-world applications demands fairness, transparency, and accountability. Picture an RL system applied in hiring processes; biases entrenched in training data could lead to unfair outcomes, harming diversity and equity. Understanding fairness has to do with vigilant scrutiny of both input data and algorithmic decisions. Transparency requires the building of models whose decision-making processes can be easily interpreted and explained. Accountability gives certainty that there's always a human in the loop to oversee and rectify potential harms caused by automated decisions. Explainable AI techniques become critically important—they create pathways for acknowledging the rationale behind decisions made by RL systems, and this can be used to check against unintended discrimination or bias.

An interesting point about RL systems is their potential to evolve continuously. However, with great power comes great responsibility. Constant updates and enhancements mean developers must stay alert to these systems so they align with new societal norms and regulations. This delicate balancing act illustrates why ethical deployment isn't just a technical issue but a broader socio-political challenge.

Simulation Environments for RL

Designing effective simulation environments for RL is like creating a vivid virtual playground where models can learn and adapt before facing the complexities of the real world. These simulated spaces must be comprehensive, offering challenges that are both diverse and representative of real-world scenarios. For instance, consider a self-driving car—in simulation, it should encounter everything from heavy traffic and adverse weather conditions to unexpected pedestrian behavior. A well-crafted simulation make sure that when these RL models transition into reality, they aren't blindsided by novel situations.

Designing Effective Simulation Environments for RL Training

When designing these environments, one rather important guideline is to imbue them with realistic dynamics and variability. This means incorporating elements like randomness and potential disruptions, which can mirror the unpredictability found in real-life situations. When doing so, RL agents can develop great adaptation strategies, making them better equipped for whatever comes their way outside of simulated walls.

Bridging the Sim-to-Real Gap in Robotics and Control Systems

One of the persistent challenges lies in bridging the gap between simulation results and real-world performance. In robotics and control systems, this is often referred to as the "sim-to-real" transfer problem. Simulations, no matter how detailed, can unintentionally simplify complex physical interactions. Take, for example, a robotic arm learning to grasp objects. While simulations might handle object properties in simplified terms, such as weight and texture, dealing with the subtleties of material deformation or friction variations is more challenging. To overcome these issues, researchers often employ techniques like domain randomization, which exposes the model to a variety of simulated environments, intentionally fluctuating key parameters so that it learns to generalize better to unseen conditions in the real world.

Parallelizing RL Training Across Multiple Simulations

Parallelization has an increasingly significant role in reinforcing learning systems, especially as the scale and complexity of problems grow. When running multiple simulations concurrently, we expedite the training process and allow for more extensive exploration of strategies and solutions. Think about a team of RL agents, each tackling slight variations of the same problem across different simulation instances. This diversity in experience speeds up the learning curve, enabling the system to sift through potential actions and consequences more efficiently. Harnessing modern computing power, particularly through cloud-based infrastructures, facilitates this level of parallelization, allowing large-scale RL training that is both feasible and practical.

Guidelines here suggest effectively leveraging cloud technologies and distributed computing resources to optimize computational efficiency. Knowing that infrastructure supports dynamic scaling can prevent bottlenecks that usually arise during peak computation periods. Proper resource management along with parallelization allows seamless scalability, which in turn allows for experiments to expand without hitting performance caps.

Validating RL Models Trained in Simulation

Validation of RL models trained in simulations is important to know if they meet real-world criteria. Before deployment, it's important to rigorously test these models against benchmarks and standards that reflect realistic expectations. This involves subjecting them to datasets and scenarios that challenge their adaptability and decision-making capabilities.

Strategies to verify these models often include stress testing, where models face unexpected changes or disturbances to assess their resilience. Alternatively, real-world pilot tests can be conducted on a smaller scale to gather valuable feedback, highlighting discrepancies between simulated and actual operations. Autonomous delivery drones tested in controlled settings provide insights on navigational precision and obstacle avoidance, revealing any oversights from simulations.

It's also worth noting the iterative nature of this validation process. Feedback loops allow continuous refinement and recalibration of models, gradually aligning their performance closer to real-world benchmarks. Just as a chef refines a recipe by tasting and adjusting ingredients, developers frequently tweak models based on run-time evaluations, closing the gap between simulation perfection and real-world application.

Quizzes and Exercises

Quiz

1. What are the main challenges in deploying reinforcement learning models in production environments?

2. Explain the exploration vs. exploitation dilemma in RL. How does this change when moving from training to production?

3. What safety considerations are crucial when implementing RL-based decision-making systems in real-world applications?

4. How does multi-agent reinforcement learning differ from single-agent RL? Provide an example scenario for each.

5. Describe the challenges in coordinating multiple agents in a cooperative multi-agent RL environment.

Exercises

1. **RL in Production:** Design an architecture for deploying a reinforcement learning model in a production environment for a specific application. Address issues of model updates, handling real-time data, and ensuring system reliability. Implement a simplified version of your design and discuss how you would scale it to a full production system.

2. **Multi-agent RL Simulation:** Implement a multi-agent reinforcement learning environment for a cooperative task (like predator-prey simulation or traffic control). Use a framework like OpenAI

Gym to create the environment. Train multiple agents to solve the task collaboratively. Analyze the emergent behaviors and discuss the challenges in scaling the system to more agents.

3. **Exploration Strategy Comparison:** Implement and compare at least three different exploration strategies in a reinforcement learning setting. Use a standard RL environment (like CartPole or MountainCar from OpenAI Gym) for your comparison. Evaluate each strategy's performance in terms of learning speed and final policy quality. Discuss how these strategies might be adapted for a production environment.

Key Insights and Practical Takeaways

- **RL in Production:** Design architectures that integrate RL models seamlessly with existing systems. Balance exploration and exploitation using techniques like epsilon-greedy strategies. Implement safety protocols and fail-safes, especially for critical applications like healthcare or autonomous vehicles.

- **Multi-Agent Systems:** Create simulated environments that mirror real-world dynamics for training multiple agents. Develop algorithms capable of both coordination and competition among agents. Address scalability challenges using parallel processing and distributed computing strategies.

- **Sample Efficiency:** Maximize learning from limited data using techniques like transfer learning. Implement advanced algorithms that make better use of available information to improve training efficiency and reduce computational load.

- **Simulation Environments:** Design comprehensive simulations that incorporate realistic variability and unpredictability. Bridge the sim-to-real gap using techniques like domain randomization. Leverage cloud technologies for parallelizing RL training across multiple simulations.

- **Ethical Considerations:** Ensure fairness, transparency, and accountability in RL system design. Implement explainable AI techniques to interpret decision-making processes. Continuously monitor and update systems to align with evolving societal norms and regulations.

CHAPTER 15

MLOps and Continuous Delivery for ML

MLOps and continuous delivery for ML are all about making sure that ML models run smoothly in production. It's about developing an impressive model as much as it is about making it function properly in the real world with minimal hiccups. In this landscape, where data is as relevant as code, integrating models into a production environment needs more than just technical know-how. It demands a systematic methodology that blends software engineering principles with data science expertise. Just imagine for a second that you're part of a team working on a big project. You've built a fantastic model, but without the right operational practices, keeping it updated and efficient could turn into a nightmare. This is where MLOps comes in. It's like having a reliable process to keep your car running great after you've put in all the hard work to build it.

In this chapter, we're exploring how MLOps can seamlessly work with continuous integration and delivery practices. You'll learn about the importance of considering both code and data dependencies to allow your models to always perform at their best. We'll look at tools and techniques that help automate these processes, reducing manual errors and speeding up workflows. There's also a focus on version control, which is essential when dealing with complex models that change over time. We'll discuss methods to allow reproducibility and scalability, which are key factors for transitioning models from small projects to large-scale applications. Plus, you'll get insights into establishing effective CI/CD systems and aligning them with ML needs to harness both efficiency and innovation. If you're looking to ace job interviews or train yourself in industry-standard practices, this chapter has the practical knowledge you need to succeed in the dynamic field of MLOps.

CI/CD Practices for ML

Adapting continuous integration and continuous delivery (CI/CD) practices to ML workflows is a fascinating arena, combining the fast-paced industry of software engineering with the demands of data science. Traditional CI/CD processes focus on code changes, but the nature of ML needs additional considerations, such as data dependencies and model training.

Adapting CI/CD Practices for ML Workflows

In a typical software project, version control and automated testing ensure smooth deployment of new features. However, when it comes to ML, data can be used as both an input and a dependency, making it important to incorporate data versioning into the CI/CD process. Say, an ML model designed to predict stock market trends. It relies on code and large datasets that need constant updating and management. Without tracking these changes meticulously, you risk unpredictable model behavior. Therefore, integrating data lifecycle management into your pipelines becomes a necessity.

Model training involves computations that go beyond traditional code compilation. It may include orchestrating various algorithms over extensive periods, sometimes across distributed systems. Here, CI/CD must evolve to manage these workload intricacies seamlessly. Automation tools like Kubernetes or Airflow can schedule and monitor long-running tasks efficiently, allowing for each iteration of model retraining to align perfectly with updated datasets and configurations. This reduces manual intervention, thereby minimizing human error and speeding up the entire process.

Automating Model Training, Evaluation, and Deployment

Automation techniques in ML drastically transform workflows by taking charge from model training to deployment. Let's say you're developing an image recognition system. Typically, this would involve multiple steps: preparing data, training the model, validating results, and deploying the model into a production environment. Automating these stages allows for consistent and rapid prototype iterations, leading to faster feedback loops and improved models. When employing automation scripts and services, organizations can maintain high accuracy and efficiency without being bogged down by repetitive tasks.

Version Control for Data, Models, and Code

Another important aspect of adapting CI/CD for ML is version control. Unlike software development, where version control focuses on code, ML demands a varied approach—covering data, model architectures, and parameters. Suppose you're working with a team spread across different locations. Making sure that everyone is on the same page requires strict adherence to versioning protocols. Tools like DVC (Data Version Control) or Git-LFS (Large File Storage) can help manage data lineage, whereas frameworks like MLflow facilitate experiment tracking and deployment workflows. This allows for transparency and reproducibility, which is very important for collaborative ML projects.

The Significance of Reproducibility

Reproducibility in ML pipelines isn't just a recommended practice; it's essential for consistency and scalability. When every team member accesses the same set of resources and instructions to train a model, the likelihood of discrepancies reduces significantly. Also, reproducible pipelines support scalability by allowing easy transitions from small-scale experiments to full-fledged industrial applications. If you're developing a sentiment analysis tool for customer feedback, having a reproducible pipeline ensures that the shift from analyzing thousands of feedback entries to millions happens smoothly and without any hiccups.

Best Practices for Reproducible ML Pipelines

Certain guidelines prove indispensable for establishing effective CI/CD systems in ML. First, embrace orchestration tools to automate every aspect of model training and deployment. Next, implement comprehensive version control strategies to handle all elements: data, models, and code. Lastly, adhere to best practices that nurture a reproducible environment, promoting seamless collaboration and scaling.

Developers who try to transition into ML roles will find the fusion of CI/CD with ML particularly enlightening. This improves operational efficiencies, but it also bridges the gap between concept and real-world application. Meanwhile, data scientists preparing for technical interviews can confidently discuss how they integrated sophisticated CI/CD methodologies into their work, demonstrating their preparedness for intricate challenges.

Adapting CI/CD practices to ML workflows highlights the need for flexibility in technological advancements. As ML continues to change rapidly, so must the methods we use to refine and deploy these models. It doesn't matter if you're striving to improve a recommendation engine or develop autonomous driving solutions; acknowledging these adaptations gives you the knowledge needed to succeed.

Model Versioning and Experiment Tracking

Going through the complex labyrinth of MLOps inevitably brings us to the concepts of versioning and experiment tracking, two important components in managing ML models effectively. Let's start with versioning, which essentially acts as a backbone for handling multiple iterations of a model. Without proper versioning practices, teams might find themselves lost in a maze when attempting to compare different versions or roll back to earlier ones after unsuccessful updates.

Tools and Techniques for Versioning ML Models

Tools like Git are often employed for code versioning, but ML models need a bit more than that. Consider using specialized tools such as DVC or MLflow, which cater specifically to data science needs. These tools help track your models, datasets, and pipelines all in one place, allowing smooth transitions between model versions. Imagine you've deployed a model only to discover later that its performance degraded due to a poorly chosen set of hyperparameters. With versioning tools in place, you can easily revert to a previous, better-performing model without much hassle.

Experiment Tracking and Management Systems

Continuing on this path, we go into experiment tracking—a critical aspect of MLOps that complements versioning. Experiment tracking systems can be used as a structured way to document every trial run, capturing details like hyperparameters, system architecture, results, and even notes on any roadblocks faced during the process. MLflow, Comet, and Weights & Biases are examples of dedicated platforms that facilitate this comprehensive recording.

These systems log details and help visualize trends, allowing teams to draw insights from past experiments. When analyzing a series of failed attempts at increasing accuracy, you might discover that tweaking a specific parameter consistently led to improvements. Such analyses allow data scientists to fine-tune models more efficiently and build upon past learnings rather than starting from scratch each time, hence optimizing resource expenditure.

Comparing and Selecting Models for Production

When it comes to selecting the ideal model for production, a clear knowledge of comparison criteria becomes indispensable. However, this task goes beyond mere performance metrics like accuracy or F1 score. It is all about considering factors such as inference latency, scalability, and reliability under various conditions. A model might perform brilliantly in controlled environments but fail to deliver when scaled up in real-time applications due to slower inference times or higher resource consumption.

Contextual factors should influence the choice of models. For example, in healthcare applications, interpretability could be prioritized over sheer performance because knowing model decisions is crucial for professionals making patient-related decisions. Thus, aligning model selection with business objectives ensures technical success and maximizes the value delivered to stakeholders.

Maintaining Model Lineage and Provenance

Another cornerstone of effective MLOps is maintaining detailed lineage and provenance of models. This practice allows for more accountability and traceability—two key elements for regulatory compliance and auditing, especially in sensitive industries like finance and healthcare. If you can establish a great lineage, teams can track how a model has evolved, what datasets were used in training, the decisions made at each phase, and who made those decisions. This clarity simplifies troubleshooting and improves transparency both internally and externally.

In maintaining model lineage, automated logging mechanisms can be a game-changer. They systematically record every stage of a model's lifecycle, creating a trail that can easily be followed. This record is a safety net when questions arise about a model's integrity or the ethical implications of its use. If an issue surfaces in production, being able to trace its roots quickly through comprehensive logs can save significant time and prevent potential reputational damage.

When it comes to this aspect, guidelines often include consistency in naming conventions across datasets, preprocessing scripts and model files, and adopting standardized templates for documentation. Implementing these practices creates an environment where knowledge transfer is seamless, thereby allowing new team members to get up to speed rapidly and contribute effectively.

Automated Testing for ML Systems

When testing ML systems, the goal is to reach reliability by employing a variety of methodologies customized to different aspects of these complex systems. Let's explore how you can systematically test ML components and functions through unit testing practices.

Unit Testing for ML Components

Unit testing in the ML context encompasses isolating and validating individual components such as data preprocessing functions, feature extraction modules, and model training algorithms. The key here is to know that each component performs its expected task accurately. For instance, you might write unit tests for a function that normalizes input data, checking whether it correctly scales features according to predefined parameters. When covering edge cases and typical scenarios, developers and ML engineers can catch bugs early in the process, ensuring a solid foundation before integrating components into larger systems.

Integration Testing for ML Pipelines

Moving from individual components, we dive into integration testing approaches that evaluate the flow and interaction of elements within the ML pipeline. Integration testing focuses on verifying that distinct parts of the pipeline when combined and function harmoniously. Picture a simple pipeline where data ingestion, feature engineering, and model prediction are sequential steps. An integration test could involve running a batch of input data through the entire pipeline, examining if data transformations and predictions yield consistent results. Through this method, potential issues arising from the interaction between pipeline stages can be identified, facilitating smoother transitions from development to production environments.

Performance and Stress Testing for ML Models

Performance and stress testing strategies can be used to assess an ML model's robustness and scalability further. These techniques help determine how models handle different loads, giving insights into their efficiency under varying conditions. Performance testing evaluates metrics like latency and throughput, pinpointing bottlenecks that could hinder real-time predictions. Stress testing pushes models to their limits by simulating high-traffic scenarios or substantial increases in data size. This helps in understanding how models might degrade in performance under pressure, allowing teams to make informed decisions about scaling resources or refining algorithms to accommodate growing demands.

A/B Testing and Shadow Deployments for ML Systems

In addition to traditional testing methods, experimentation with live systems through A/B testing and shadow deployments provides avenues for safe innovation. A/B testing divides traffic between two versions of a model, comparing metrics such as accuracy and user engagement to decide which version performs better. This method allows for controlled experimentation, minimizing risks associated with deploying unproven changes. Meanwhile, shadow deployments involve running a new model alongside the current one without impacting end users. If you analyze outputs in parallel, you can monitor real-world behavior and gather valuable feedback before permanently switching. Together, these techniques increase decision-making processes, enabling organizations to refine models iteratively while reducing unforeseen disruptions to live operations.

If you incorporate these testing methodologies, you create a solid framework for developing reliable ML systems. Effective unit testing sets the groundwork by catching errors at the smallest level. Integration testing allows for seamless collaboration between components, addressing potential flaws in connected systems. Performance and stress testing reveal limitations and prepares models for the dynamic demands of production environments. Finally, A/B testing and shadow deployments promote an experimental culture, encouraging continuous improvement based on data-driven insights.

Monitoring and Observability in Production

MLOps, knowing that your models in production continue to perform as expected is quite relevant. One of the main aspects of this is monitoring, a practice that helps maintain reliability and effectiveness over time. Let's get into how to set up effective monitoring for production ML models, starting with a look at key metrics.

Key Metrics for Monitoring ML Systems

When it comes to monitoring ML systems, identifying the right metrics is foundational. Latency, throughput, and error rates are some of the primary indicators to focus on. Latency measures the time delay in processing requests by your model, which directly affects the user experience. High latency can indicate issues like inefficient model computations or resource bottlenecks. Throughput tells us how many requests our model handles successfully over a period; a drop might signify performance degradation due to increased load or environmental changes. Error rates highlight failures in processing requests correctly, perhaps due to data drift or unexpected input types. Recognizing these metrics allows engineers to quickly identify potential problems and optimize systems accordingly.

Detecting and Diagnosing Issues in Production ML Models

Observability tools are invaluable when it comes to detecting and diagnosing issues in production models. These tools provide insights into the internal workings of your models, offering visibility into behavior patterns and system states. Methods such as log analysis, distributed tracing, and metric aggregation are quite significant here. Log analysis can help track anomalies by examining records of operational information, while distributed tracing provides end-to-end tracking of requests across services in microservice architectures. Metric aggregation tools compile performance data, allowing trend identification over time. Using these techniques together can lead to swift issue detection and resolution, minimizing downtime and impact on users.

Implementing Alerting and Reporting Mechanisms

An integral component of effective monitoring is an alerting and reporting framework. Having a structured way to notify relevant stakeholders about emerging issues ensures that any problems are addressed promptly. Establish alerts based on defined thresholds for key metrics—these could be simple notifications for minor deviations or escalation procedures for severe disruptions. A reporting system should also include routine performance summaries, helping teams analyze trends and adjust strategies proactively. When implemented correctly, these frameworks speed up problem-solving and promote better communication within and across teams.

Techniques for Model Interpretability and Explainability in Production

Enhancing model interpretability and explainability is quite relevant here, especially in production environments where decisions often need to be justified. Techniques such as SHAP (SHapley Additive exPlanations) values and LIME (Local Interpretable Model-agnostic Explanations) give ways to unpack model predictions and understand feature importance. If adopting these methods, you can demystify black-box models and make informed decisions, which is increasingly important in sectors like finance and healthcare, where regulatory compliance demands transparency. Interpretable models build stakeholder trust, providing assurance that predictions align with business objectives and ethical guidelines.

Each of these aspects forms a pillar of great monitoring in MLOps. Identifying and using the right metrics gives a clear picture of model health, while observability tools provide teams to catch and fix issues before they escalate. Effective alerting and reporting keep everyone in the loop, preventing small hitches from turning into significant bottlenecks. Lastly, interpretability makes sure that all involved parties can trust and rely on ML outputs.

Quizzes and Exercises

Quiz

1. How does CI/CD for machine learning differ from traditional software CI/CD? What additional considerations are needed?

2. Explain the importance of version control for data in ML workflows. How does it differ from code version control?

3. What are the key components of a reproducible ML pipeline? How do they contribute to the reproducibility of experiments?

4. Describe the concept of model lineage. Why is it crucial in MLOps?

5. What are some common tools used for experiment tracking in ML projects? What features make them suitable for ML workflows?

Exercises

1. **CI/CD Pipeline for ML:** Design and implement a CI/CD pipeline for a ML project. Your pipeline should include stages for data validation, model training, testing, and deployment. Use tools like Jenkins, GitLab CI, or GitHub Actions to automate the pipeline. Demonstrate how your pipeline handles changes in data, model code, and hyperparameters.

2. **Model Versioning and Experiment Tracking:** Set up an experiment tracking system for an ML project using a tool like MLflow, Weights & Biases, or DVC. Conduct a series of experiments with different model architectures, hyperparameters, and datasets. Use the system to track and compare the results of your experiments. Demonstrate how you would use this system to select the best model for production.

3. **Automated Testing Suite:** Develop a comprehensive testing suite for an ML pipeline. Include unit tests for data preprocessing functions, model components, and evaluation metrics. Implement integration tests that verify the entire pipeline from data ingestion to model output. Create performance tests that check the model's accuracy and latency under various conditions. Use a testing framework like pytest and integrate it into your CI/CD pipeline.

Key Insights and Practical Takeaways

- **CI/CD for ML:** Adapt traditional CI/CD practices to include data versioning and model training pipelines. Use tools like Kubernetes or Airflow to automate and orchestrate long-running ML tasks. Implement version control for data, models, and code using specialized tools like DVC or MLflow.

- **Model Versioning and Experiment Tracking:** Utilize dedicated platforms like MLflow, Comet, or Weights & Biases to track experiments, compare model versions, and maintain model lineage. Consider factors beyond performance metrics, such as inference latency and scalability, when selecting models for production.

- **Automated Testing for ML:** Implement comprehensive testing strategies, including unit tests for individual ML components, integration tests for pipelines, and performance/stress tests to assess model robustness. Use A/B testing and shadow deployments to safely experiment with new models in live environments.

- **Monitoring and Observability:** Set up monitoring systems to track key metrics like latency, throughput, and error rates. Implement observability tools for log analysis, distributed tracing, and metric aggregation. Establish alerting mechanisms and reporting frameworks to quickly identify and address issues in production.

- **Model Interpretability:** Adopt techniques like SHAP values and LIME to enhance model explainability, especially in regulated industries. Prioritize transparency to build stakeholder trust and ensure alignment with business objectives and ethical guidelines.

BOOK 3

Mastering the ML System Design Interview

CHAPTER 16

Interview Preparation Strategies

Preparing for ML system design interviews can feel like stepping into a whole new world of challenges and opportunities. These interviews are a lot about assessing your technical skills; they really go into how you think, solve problems, and communicate solutions effectively. The goal is to show interviewers that you're knowledgeable but also creative and adaptable in your approach. You have a chance to show how you break down complex issues into manageable parts and come up with new strategies that could set you apart from other candidates. Your problem-solving techniques, ability to design scalable systems, and understanding of trade-offs are relevant in illustrating your competency in this field. Striking the right balance between showing off your technical expertise and clearly communicating your ideas is key to leaving a memorable impression.

Here, we will go into different strategies to help you prepare for these demanding interviews. We will talk about what interviewers generally look for, including problem-solving capabilities, out-of-the-box thinking, and the ability to design systems that handle scalability efficiently. We'll also discuss the importance of knowing and articulating trade-offs in your designs, as well as balancing technical proficiency with effective communication skills. The chapter will further guide you on how to showcase both broad knowledge and specialized expertise during the interview process. To give you a real edge, we'll cover tips on conducting mock interviews to improve your presentation abilities and advice on keeping up-to-date with industry trends to make your answers more compelling. Regardless of what you do, either a software engineer transitioning into ML roles, a data scientist preparing for a technical interview, or a student eager to enter the ML field, this chapter is packed with practical insights customized to help you excel.

Understanding the Interviewer's Perspective

ML system design interviews are a different type of challenge, as they go into the thought processes and technical prowess of candidates. Knowing exactly what interviewers look for is important to succeeding in these interviews. First and foremost, problem-solving skills are at the forefront of qualities sought by interviewers. They want to see how you regard complex problems, break them down into manageable components, and devise efficient solutions.

Preparation Steps:

1. Study common ML system design problems (e.g., recommendation systems, fraud detection, image recognition).

2. Practice breaking down complex problems into manageable components.

Exercise:

- Choose a complex ML system (e.g., Netflix's recommendation engine) and spend 30 minutes outlining its main components and how they interact.

- Set a timer for 10 minutes and brainstorm as many innovative solutions as possible for a given problem (e.g., reducing latency in a large-scale image classification system).

Common Evaluation Criteria Used by Top Tech Companies

In addition to these qualities, top tech companies have specific evaluation criteria for assessing candidates.

Designing Scalable Systems

One common criterion is how well you can design scalable systems. Interviewers assess your ability to address scalability concerns, making sure that your system can handle increasing loads efficiently.

Exercise:

- Take an existing ML model you're familiar with and outline how you would scale it to handle 100x more data and users.

- Create a checklist of scalability considerations (e.g., data storage, model training, inference speed) to review during interviews.

Understanding Trade-Offs

To add to that, acknowledging trade-offs is essential. Companies look for candidates who can make informed decisions about the pros and cons of different methodologies, particularly when it comes to balancing performance and resource utilization.

Preparation Steps:

1. Create a list of common ML trade-offs (e.g., accuracy vs. speed, model complexity vs. interpretability).

2. Practice explaining these trade-offs in simple terms.

Exercise:

- For each trade-off, write a brief explanation and an example of when you might choose one option over the other.

- Conduct a mock interview where you explain a trade-off decision you made in a past project.

Finding the Balance

Another key aspect is the candidate's ability to strike a balance between showcasing technical proficiency and effective communication skills. You might be technically sound, but if you're unable to convey your ideas clearly, it could be detrimental. To achieve this balance, it's important to practice articulating your thoughts systematically. Start by explaining your thought process clearly at each step, and back up your assertions with evidence or examples whenever possible. Remember, clarity is crucial, both in written and verbal explanations.

Preparation Steps:

1. Practice explaining complex ML concepts to nontechnical friends or family.

2. Record yourself explaining an ML system design and review for clarity and conciseness.

Exercise:

- Choose an ML concept and create three explanations: one for a peer, one for a manager, and one for a client. Focus on adjusting your language and depth for each audience.

How to Demonstrate Both Breadth and Depth of Knowledge

Presenting both broad knowledge and in-depth expertise is another expectation in ML system design interviews. While it's important to show a solid understanding of various ML concepts and technologies, having specialized knowledge in certain areas can set you apart. You might have a broad knowledge of neural networks, but being an expert in convolutional neural networks (CNNs) for image recognition showcases depth. The trick is to seamlessly weave these together during interviews.

Preparation Steps:

1. Create a knowledge map of ML topics, highlighting your areas of expertise.

2. Regularly read ML research papers and blog posts to stay updated.

Exercise:

- Choose a broad ML topic (e.g., neural networks) and dive deep into a specific subtopic (e.g., CNNs for image recognition). Prepare a 5-minute presentation that covers both the broad concept and your deep dive.

- Set up a weekly "Learn and Share" session with peers where each person presents on a different ML topic.

Examples of How to Show Breadth and Depth of Knowledge

To illustrate effective demonstration strategies, imagine you're asked to design a recommendation system. A good way to go about it would be first to outline the general steps involved, such as data collection, pre-processing, model selection, and evaluation metrics. Then, venture deeper into specifics, like discussing collaborative filtering methods or content-based filtering, showing off both breadth and depth. Throughout your explanation, maintain a coherent narrative that ties all elements together logically.

Preparation Steps:

1. Study case studies of ML systems deployed by major tech companies.

2. Practice identifying potential challenges and constraints in real-world ML applications.

Exercise:

- Choose a real-world ML application (e.g., autonomous vehicles, voice assistants) and spend an hour outlining potential challenges, constraints, and solutions.

- Conduct a mock interview where you're given new information midway through your design explanation. Practice adapting your design on the spot.

Balancing Technical Skills With Communication Abilities

When preparing for these interviews, keep in mind that demonstrating soft skills is just as important as showcasing technical skills. Effective collaboration and teamwork are quite important in the success of any project. During system design interviews, articulate your willingness to work with others, but also showcase your ability to take initiative when needed.

Preparation Steps:
1. Join or create an ML study group to practice collaboration.
2. Seek opportunities to present your ML projects or research to diverse audiences.

Exercise:
- Participate in an ML hackathon or competition as part of a team.
- Practice active listening: In your next conversation about ML, focus on asking follow-up questions and summarizing what others say before responding.

Common Interview Formats

When preparing for ML system design interviews, it's really important that you know the different interview formats you may encounter. Generally, these interviews can be divided into two categories: open-ended questions and specific problem-solving scenarios. Open-ended questions allow candidates to showcase their creativity and depth of knowledge by posing broad challenges without a predetermined solution. For example, you might be asked to design a recommendation system from scratch. Here, interviewers assess how well you break down complex problems, explore various angles, and prioritize solutions based on given constraints.

Open-Ended vs. Specific Problem-Solving Questions

Specific problem-solving scenarios require candidates to address defined issues with clear expectations. Such tasks might involve optimizing an existing model's efficiency or integrating a new component into a ML pipeline. These scenarios test your problem-solving ability and your technical expertise and familiarity with industry-standard tools and techniques.

Open-Ended Questions

Format Overview: Broad challenges without predetermined solutions, testing creativity and problem-solving skills.

Preparation Steps:

1. Study diverse ML case studies across industries.

2. Practice breaking down complex systems into components.

Exercises:

- Weekly System Breakdown: Choose a popular ML-powered product (e.g., Spotify's music recommender or Google's image search). Spend 30 minutes outlining its potential architecture, components, and ML models used.

- Constraint Challenge: Pick an ML system and add imaginary constraints (e.g., limited compute resources, strict latency requirements). Spend 20 minutes adapting your design to these constraints.

Specific Problem-Solving Scenarios

Format Overview: Defined issues with clear expectations, testing technical expertise and familiarity with ML tools.

Preparation Steps:

1. Review common ML optimization techniques.

2. Practice implementing ML pipelines using industry-standard tools.

Exercises:

- Daily LeetCode: Solve one ML-related problem on LeetCode or HackerRank daily. Focus on algorithmic efficiency and clean code.

- Pipeline Optimization: Choose an existing ML pipeline (e.g., from a Kaggle competition). Spend 1 hour identifying and implementing at least three optimizations.

Whiteboard Design Sessions and Their Dynamics

Whiteboard design sessions are another common element of ML system design interviews. In these settings, you're expected to physically sketch out your ideas on a whiteboard while clearly explaining your thought process to the interviewer. This dynamic is particularly insightful for employers as it showcases your ability to conceptualize and communicate complex concepts on the spot.

Format Overview: Real-time system design and explanation using a whiteboard, testing conceptualization, and communication skills.

Preparation Steps:

1. Practice drawing clear, organized diagrams of ML systems.

2. Develop a structured approach to explaining your design process.

Exercises:

- Whiteboard Wednesdays: Weekly 1-hour sessions with a study partner. Take turns presenting ML system designs on a whiteboard (or digital equivalent). Provide feedback to each other on clarity and completeness.

- 5-Minute Explainer: Regularly practice explaining complex ML concepts in 5 minutes or less. Record yourself and review for clarity and conciseness.

Remote Interview Considerations and Best Practices

With the rise of remote work, virtual interviews have become increasingly prevalent. Remote interviews introduce new challenges, such as having stable internet connectivity and managing digital tools efficiently.

Format Overview: Virtual interviews using video conferencing and digital collaboration tools.

Preparation Steps:

1. Set up a professional home office space for interviews.

2. Familiarize yourself with common video conferencing and digital whiteboard tools.

Get Familiar With Your Software: One effective strategy for these interviews is to familiarize yourself with the video conferencing platform being used. Make sure your audio and video equipment is working properly, and be prepared to share screens when needed.

Communication: This is everything in remote interviews. Without the benefit of physical presence, tone and clarity of speech become even more important. Practicing concise and structured communication will make sure your points are understood despite any technological hiccups that may occur. It's beneficial to pause momentarily after making significant points, inviting the interviewer to provide feedback or ask clarifying questions, which can help maintain engagement and understanding throughout the conversation.

Adaptation: Adapting your preparation methods to fit each interview format and environment is critical. For open-ended questions, immerse yourself in case studies and real-world applications of ML. Knowing how various algorithms and models are employed across industries can give you a richer context for discussions. Also, keeping up-to-date with current trends and advancements in the field allows you to bring fresh insights to the table.

Practice: For specific problem-solving scenarios, hands-on practice with coding exercises and algorithm challenges is invaluable. Sites like LeetCode or HackerRank offer numerous examples that can simulate the types of tasks you might face. When practicing, try to explain your logic aloud, as though you're speaking to an audience. This will help you get used to verbalizing your thought process during actual interviews.

Get Familiar with Standard Design Patterns: To excel in whiteboard sessions, familiarize yourself with standard design patterns and architectural frameworks within ML systems. Gaining comfort with diagramming workflows and data flows will bolster your ability to present coherent designs under pressure. Engaging regularly in informal group discussions where you debate design choices can also sharpen your abilities to think on your feet and defend your decisions convincingly.

Create a Routine: When preparing for remote interviews, create a routine that includes trial runs of the technology you'll be using. Practice in a similar setting to what the interview will be like, knowing that everything from sound levels to screen-sharing capabilities is smooth. Simulate full-length interviews with friends or mentors who can provide feedback on content and delivery.

Cross-Format Exercises:

1. **ML News Discussion Group:**
    - Form a weekly group to discuss recent ML advancements and their potential applications.
    - Take turns presenting a news item and leading a 15-minute discussion on its implications.

2. **Design Pattern Flashcards:**
    - Create flashcards for common ML system design patterns and architectures.

- Review them regularly, practicing quick sketches and explanations for each.

3. **Rapid Fire Q&A:**
    - With a study partner, take turns asking and answering common ML interview questions.
    - Focus on giving concise, clear answers within 2-3 minutes.

4. **System Design Journal:**
    - Keep a journal of ML systems you encounter in daily life (e.g., recommendation systems, voice assistants).
    - Regularly spend 15 minutes hypothesizing about their potential architectures and challenges.

5. **Mock Interview Marathon:**
    - Once a month, schedule a day of back-to-back mock interviews in various formats.
    - Recruit friends, mentors, or online practice partners to play different interviewer roles.

Key Areas of Assessment

With ML system design interviews, candidates are expected to show a set of core competencies. The foundation of these assessments is an individual's technical prowess, particularly in acknowledging and applying ML algorithms and system architecture principles. For software engineers transitioning into ML roles, this means moving beyond basic coding skills to grasp how various ML models operate, their strengths and limitations, and how they integrate into larger systems. A solid comprehension of concepts like supervised and unsupervised learning, neural networks, or reinforcement learning can significantly impact your ability to stand out.

Problem-Solving and Analytical Thinking Skills

Consider a scenario where you're asked to design a recommendation system. It's about picking the right algorithm and understanding why it suits the specific problem. Would collaborative filtering or a content-based approach be more effective? How would this system scale with increased data flow? These questions highlight the need for solid technical knowledge that goes beyond theoretical knowledge. Also, understanding system architecture helps in designing frameworks that support scalability, reliability, and efficiency—the main aspects companies look for when evaluating candidates.

Focus: Clearly convey complex ideas, actively listen, and work effectively in a team.

Preparation Steps:

1. Practice decomposing ML problems into smaller, manageable parts.

2. Develop a structured approach to analyzing ML system performance.

Exercises:

- Weekly Case Study Analysis: Choose a real-world ML application. Spend 1 hour analyzing its potential challenges and proposing solutions. Document your thought process.

- Performance Optimization Challenge: Select an ML model and dataset. Spend 2 hours improving its performance. Document each step, the reasoning behind it, and its impact.

Ability to Make Trade-Offs and Justify Design Decisions

Equally important is the capacity to make informed trade-offs and justify design decisions. Within ML, not every choice is black and white. Models may need to balance accuracy against computational cost or prioritize speed over precision, depending on the context. Let's consider a case where you're tasked with developing a real-time fraud detection system. You might have to decide between using a sophisticated deep learning model that offers high accuracy but with latency versus a simpler model that processes transactions faster. Articulating why you chose one way over another is where the guideline becomes relevant.

Focus: Balancing competing priorities, making informed decisions, and articulating rationales.

Preparation Steps:

1. Study common trade-offs in ML systems (e.g., accuracy vs. speed, complexity vs. interpretability).

2. Practice explaining your decision-making process clearly and concisely.

Exercises:

- Trade-Off Scenarios: Create a list of 10 ML system design scenarios with conflicting requirements. Spend 15 minutes on each, deciding on a solution and writing a brief justification.

- Decision Tree Exercise: For a complex ML system design decision, create a decision tree outlining different options, their pros and cons, and potential outcomes. Present your analysis to a peer or mentor.

Communication and Collaboration Capabilities

Finally, communication and collaboration abilities hold significant weight in system design interviews. While individual brilliance is valuable, the ability to work within a team is equally important. Projects in real-world settings demand collaboration and leveraging diverse skill sets to achieve success. Hence, interviewers assess how well you can convey your ideas and absorb others' inputs.

Focus: Clearly conveying complex ideas, active listening, and working effectively in a team.

Preparation Steps:
1. Practice explaining ML concepts to nontechnical audiences.
2. Develop skills in creating clear, informative diagrams of ML systems.

Exercises:
- Whiteboard Explanation Sessions: Weekly 30-minute sessions with a partner. Take turns explaining ML concepts or system designs on a whiteboard. Provide feedback to each other on clarity and engagement.
- ML Concept Simplification: Choose a complex ML concept weekly. Create three explanations: one for a child, one for a nontechnical adult, and one for a technical peer. Each explanation should be under 2 minutes.

Effective Communication Techniques

In preparing for ML system design interviews, one good skill to have is the ability to communicate ideas clearly and effectively. This begins with structuring your thoughts in a coherent manner. Say you're asked to design a recommendation system. Rather than going directly into technical details; first, break down your response into digestible parts: Start with an overview of the problem, outline potential solutions, weigh their pros and cons, and finally, give your preferred solution with justified reasoning. When you follow this organized approach, you can show clarity and precision in your responses, making them easier for interviewers to follow. It's also helpful to practice this structuring with different scenarios before the interview, so it becomes second nature.

Using Diagrams and Visualizations Effectively

Visual aids like diagrams can be powerful tools to complement your verbal explanations. They help convey complex concepts succinctly and are particularly helpful when describing system architectures or data flow. If you're explaining how a convolutional neural network processes images, sketching out the layers can provide a visual reference that makes your explanation more tangible.

Goal: Enhance explanations with clear, effective visual aids.

Exercise: 60 Seconds Sketch Challenge

1. List 10 core ML concepts or system components (e.g., CNN architecture, recommendation system flow).

2. For each item, set 60 seconds on the timer.

3. Quickly sketch a diagram explaining the concept.

4. Spend two minutes refining and practicing how you'd verbally explain the sketch.

Weekly Visualization Project:

- Choose a complex ML system (e.g., autonomous driving, language translation).

- Create a comprehensive visual representation of its architecture.

- Present your diagram to a peer, explaining each component in detail.

Asking Clarifying Questions and Managing Assumptions

Being able to ask clarifying questions is another relevant aspect of effective communication. Interviews often pose problems that may appear ambiguous or open-ended, intentionally testing your ability to address assumptions and gather necessary information. If tasked with designing a sentiment analysis tool, you might ask about specifics such as the scope of languages, the context in which it will be used, or the expected user base. These questions help clarify expectations and showcase your ability to think critically about the task at hand. Knowing that asking questions isn't a sign of weakness but a demonstration of thoroughness can greatly improve your performance in interviews.

Goal: Demonstrate critical thinking and gather necessary information.

Exercise: Question Formulation Technique (QFT)

1. Take an ambiguous ML system design prompt (e.g., "Design a content moderation system").

2. Spend 3 minutes writing down as many questions as possible about the prompt.

3. Categorize your questions (e.g., technical, business requirements, constraints).

4. Prioritize the top 5 most critical questions.

5. Practice asking these questions concisely and professionally.

Role-Play Activity:
- Partner with a peer for a 20-minute session.
- One person plays the interviewer, providing a vague ML design challenge.
- The other asks clarifying questions to gather information.
- Switch roles and repeat.

Handling Feedback and Iterating on Your Designs

Handling feedback constructively is vital in iterating your designs based on interviewer input. During interviews, you might receive immediate feedback about your proposed solution, either through questions or direct comments. Embrace this feedback positively, viewing it as an opportunity to refine your design. If an interviewer points out a flaw or suggests an alternative method, take a moment to consider their perspective. You might decide to adjust your model accordingly or give a justification for sticking with your initial plan. Demonstrating flexibility and a willingness to integrate feedback can reinforce your collaborative skills, and make a lasting impression on interview panels.

Goal: Demonstrate flexibility and collaborative problem-solving.

Exercise: Feedback Integration Simulation

1. Present an initial ML system design to a peer (15 minutes).

2. Have your peer provide constructive feedback and suggestions (5 minutes).

3. Spend 10 minutes adjusting your design based on the feedback.

4. Re-present your updated design, explaining the changes and your reasoning (10 minutes).

Iterative Design Journal:
- Start a design journal for an ML project (personal or hypothetical).

- Each week, add an entry detailing:
  - Current design state
  - Feedback received (from peers, mentors, or self-reflection)
  - Planned iterations and justifications

Interview Day Checklist

- **Pre-Interview Preparation:** Review the job description and company information. Prepare questions for the interviewer about the role and company. Review your resume and be prepared to discuss any project or experience. Get a good night's sleep.

- **Technical Preparation:** Review key ML concepts and algorithms. Practice system design fundamentals. Prepare a mental framework for approaching design problems. Review recent projects or case studies you might want to reference.

- **Materials to Bring:** Several copies of your resume. Notepad and pen. Portfolio of projects (if applicable). Any requested documents (ID, references, etc.).

- **For Virtual Interviews:** Test your computer, camera, and microphone. Ensure a stable internet connection. Set up a professional background. Have the interview link and software ready.

- **Personal Preparation:** Dress appropriately for the company culture. Plan to arrive 15 minutes early (or log in 5–10 minutes early for virtual interviews). Bring a water bottle. Take deep breaths and use relaxation techniques to calm nerves.

- **Post-Interview:** Prepare to send a thank-you email within 24 hours. Make notes about the interview experience for future reference. Plan your follow-up strategy if you haven't heard back within the specified timeframe.

Quizzes and Exercises

Quiz

1. What are three key things that interviewers typically look for in ML system design candidates?

2. How does an open-ended system design question differ from a specific problem-solving question?

3. Why is it important to balance technical skills with communication abilities in an ML system design interview?

4. What are some effective ways to demonstrate depth of knowledge without overwhelming the interviewer?

5. Describe the typical structure of a whiteboard design session in an ML system design interview.

Exercises

1. **Mock Interview Simulation:** Pair up with a study partner or mentor. Have them play the role of an interviewer and present you with an ML system design problem. Go through a full 45-minute interview session, including problem clarification, system design, and Q&A. After the session, ask for feedback on your performance, focusing on both technical content and communication style.

2. **Whiteboard Practice:** Choose an ML system design problem (like "Design a real-time fraud detection system for a bank"). Practice explaining your design approach on a whiteboard or digital drawing tool. Focus on clearly structuring your thoughts, using appropriate diagrams, and verbally explaining your design choices. If possible, record yourself and review it, to identify areas for improvement in your presentation.

3. **Trade-off Analysis:** For a given ML system requirement (such as "The model needs to make predictions in under 100ms"), list out at least three possible approaches to meet this requirement. For each approach, identify the pros and cons, considering factors like scalability, cost, and complexity. Practice articulating these trade-offs as you would in an interview setting.

Key Insights and Practical Takeaways

- **Understanding Interviewer Perspective:** Focus on demonstrating problem-solving skills, innovative thinking, and the ability to design scalable systems. Balance showcasing technical proficiency with effective communication. Prepare to discuss trade-offs in your design decisions.

- **Interview Formats:** Be ready for both open-ended questions and specific problem-solving scenarios. Practice whiteboard design sessions to improve your ability to conceptualize and communicate complex ideas. For remote interviews, ensure your technical setup is reliable and practice clear, concise communication.

- **Key Assessment Areas:** Develop strong technical knowledge in ML algorithms and system architecture. Hone your analytical thinking and problem-solving skills. Be prepared to make and justify trade-offs in your designs. Demonstrate effective communication and collaboration capabilities.

- **Communication Techniques:** Structure your thoughts coherently when explaining solutions. Use diagrams and visualizations to illustrate complex concepts. Ask clarifying questions and manage assumptions effectively. Handle feedback positively and be willing to iterate on your designs.

- **Preparation Strategies:** Conduct mock interviews to improve presentation skills. Stay updated with industry trends and emerging technologies. Practice explaining your thought process aloud. Familiarize yourself with standard ML design patterns and architectural frameworks.

CHAPTER 17

Problem-Solving Framework

Tackling ML system design problems can feel like solving a complex puzzle. You have all these pieces—algorithms, data pipelines, evaluation methods—and the goal is to fit them together seamlessly to create an efficient and effective solution. The process can be daunting, especially in interview settings where you need to articulate each step clearly and confidently. But here's the good news: With a structured approach, you can transform these challenges into manageable tasks. Understanding how to deconstruct problems and focus on main components first, allows you to lay a solid foundation for tackling even the most intimidating design questions.

So, here, we will first introduce a problem-solving framework that guides you through designing ML systems methodically. Beginning with decomposition strategies, and then showing you how you can break down large problems into smaller parts, makes them easier to handle. Then, we'll look at how prioritizing functionalities based on their importance keeps your project on track, making sure key features are delivered without getting sidetracked by less critical elements. We'll also discuss iterative enhancement—a technique that involves starting simple and building complexity over time, which allows you to continuously improve based on feedback. Finally, we'll talk about systematic evaluation techniques and guidelines that help assess your design's effectiveness, giving you clear metrics to judge its success. This framework increases your ability to solve ML design problems and gives you practical skills that are beneficial during technical interviews.

Step-by-Step Approach to ML System Design Problems

When faced with ML system design challenges, having a structured approach can make the difference between success and confusion. Let's look into how you can tackle these complex issues with ease, starting with decomposition.

Decomposition is all about breaking down large, intimidating problems into smaller, more manageable parts. Think of it like handling a giant jigsaw puzzle: Focusing on separate sections makes the task less overwhelming. If tasked with designing an ML recommendation engine, begin by acknowledging main components such as data collection, feature selection, model training, and evaluation. Each component needs its own set of solutions and resources. When you isolate these tasks, you can prioritize effectively and address each segment systematically. This helps in managing cognitive load and gives you clarity on the resources and time needed for each part.

Problem Decomposition

Action: Break down the large problem into smaller, manageable components.

Example: Designing a product recommendation engine for an e-commerce platform

- Components:

    a. Data collection and preprocessing

    b. Feature engineering

    c. Model selection and training

    d. Recommendation generation

    e. Evaluation and feedback loop

Tip: Create a visual diagram (e.g., flowchart) of your components to clarify their relationships and dependencies.

Prioritization of Functional Requirements

Next, let's talk about the prioritization of functional requirements. In any ML project, there are must-have features and nice-to-have ones. It's fundamental to pinpoint relevant functionalities that align closely with the problem at hand. Say you're working on a sentiment analysis tool; your primary focus should be on accurately classifying sentiments rather than adding extraneous features like real-time processing, which might come later.

Action: Identify and rank the most critical features of your ML system.

Example: For a sentiment analysis tool for social media posts

   a. Accurate sentiment classification (positive, negative, neutral)

   b. Multi-language support

   c. Handling of Emojis and hashtags

   d. Real-time processing (nice-to-have)

Tip: Use a prioritization matrix (importance vs. effort) to visually plot your features and decide what to focus on first.

Interactive Enhancement

Iterative enhancement is another relevant piece of the puzzle. Start small with a basic version of your solution. This "minimum viable product" method allows for quick testing and feedback. Let's say you're developing a chatbot; initially, it may only respond to simple queries. Based on user interaction and feedback, you can iteratively add complexity, such as knowing context or sophisticated intent recognition. This cycle of building, testing, and refining builds confidence in your design choices and allows for continual improvement. It also mimics the natural evolution of ML systems in real-world applications, where ongoing adjustments are made in response to new data and shifting requirements.

Action: Start with a basic version and incrementally add complexity.

Example: Developing a chatbot for customer service

- Iteration 1: Simple keyword-based responses

- Iteration 2: Intent recognition using ML

- Iteration 3: Contextual understanding and memory

- Iteration 4: Integration with backend systems for personalized responses

Tip: Set clear goals for each iteration and gather user feedback to guide improvements.

Guidelines to Streamline Systematic Processes

Introducing guidelines can help streamline this systematic process. A step-by-step method benefits those tackling ML system design challenges, especially when preparing for interviews. Begin by defining the problem clearly, followed by breaking it down into understandable segments. Prioritize functionalities based on their impact and necessity, create a baseline prototype, and continuously refine it while assessing each iteration against predefined criteria. This structured methodology improves your ability to solve problems efficiently and showcases your thought process, which is vital in interview settings.

Taking these steps provides a tactical advantage in approaching ML system design. Decomposition allows for targeted solutions, prioritization allows alignment with fundamental needs, iterations offer pathways for continuous refinement, and systematic evaluations validate your design's effectiveness. When you adopt these practices, you'll be able to go through ML projects more deftly, but also prepare yourself thoroughly for the demands and expectations of technical interviews.

Action: Establish specific criteria and metrics for assessing each component.

Example: Evaluating a fraud detection system for a financial institution

- Model performance: Precision, recall, F1 score
- System performance: Latency, throughput
- Business impact: False positive rate, cost savings

Tip: Create a dashboard that tracks these metrics over time to visualize progress and identify areas for improvement.

Guidelines

- **Define the problem:** Clearly state the objective and constraints of your ML system.
    - Tip: Write a one-sentence problem statement and list 3–5 key constraints.
- **Sketch the high-level architecture:** Draw a block diagram of the main components.
    - Tip: Use tools like draw.io or Lucidchart for quick, shareable diagrams.

- **Deep dive into each component:** For each block in your architecture:
    - Describe its function
    - Outline potential ML algorithms or techniques
    - Discuss data requirements
    - **Tip:** Create a table with columns for each of these aspects for easy reference.
- **Address scalability and robustness:** Consider how your system will handle growth and edge cases.
    - **Tip:** Conduct a "What If" analysis: What if the data volume doubles? What if a component fails?
- **Propose an implementation plan:** Outline the steps to bring your design to life.
    - **Tip:** Use a Gantt chart to visualize the timeline and dependencies of your implementation phases.

Clarifying Requirements

When getting into the ML system design, especially in the context of interviews, knowing what is truly needed becomes relevant. This step is foundational and has to do with getting to grips with explicit needs—what the system must achieve and the real constraints it operates within. Suppose you're building a recommendation engine for an e-commerce site—the primary need might be to suggest relevant products to users based on their browsing history. However, this system also needs to function efficiently under load, respect user privacy, and integrate smoothly with existing technology. These are your explicit needs.

Key Point: Identify explicit needs and constraints of the ML system.

Example: Building a recommendation engine for an e-commerce site.

- Primary need: Suggest relevant products based on browsing history.
- Constraints: Efficient under load, respect user privacy, integrate with existing tech.

Actionable Tips:
- Create a checklist of must-have features vs. nice-to-have features.

- Use the SMART criteria (Specific, Measurable, Achievable, Relevant, Time-bound) to define requirements.

- Develop user stories to capture functional requirements from the end-user perspective.

Effective Stakeholder Communication

Once you understand this, the next main part of the puzzle is engaging in effective stakeholder communication. It's about aligning your goals with those of others who have a vested interest in the ML system, such as product managers, engineers, or clients. Communication here isn't just about talking but also about actively listening and making sure that everyone is on the same page concerning objectives and expectations. Suppose the stakeholders from the marketing team emphasize that the recommendation engine should double the conversion rate. In that case, you have to keep those expectations aligned with technological possibilities and limitations. This ongoing dialogue helps avoid misunderstandings and reveals insights that might influence technical decisions.

Key Point: Align goals with all parties involved in the ML system.

Example: Marketing team expects the recommendation engine to double conversion rate.

Actionable Tips:

- Schedule regular check-ins with stakeholders (e.g., weekly stand-ups)

- Use a RACI matrix (Responsible, Accountable, Consulted, Informed) to clarify roles and communication channels

- Prepare a one-page executive summary of the project for quick alignment checks

- Use visual aids (diagrams, charts) in presentations to convey complex ideas simply

Documentation of Goals and Assumptions

A critical component of orchestrating this alignment is through diligent documentation of goals and assumptions. This documentation acts as a blueprint, providing clarity and direction throughout the design process. This can be used as a reference point, detailing what has been agreed upon and the assumptions made regarding data availability, system latency, or user interaction models.

Let's say there's an assumption that the user data needed for recommendations will be consistently updated every 24 hours. If this assumption changes at any point, having a well-documented record allows the necessary adjustments to be made without derailing the project. Documentation guides the design phase and this allows you to maintain focus and accountability among team members and stakeholders.

Key Point: Create a blueprint for clarity and direction throughout the design process.

Example: Documenting the assumption that user data will be updated every 24 hours.

Actionable Tips:

- Create a living document (e.g., in a wiki or shared document) for goals and assumptions.
- Use a standardized template for documenting assumptions, including:
    - Assumption description
    - Impact on the project
    - Validation method
    - Owner responsible for tracking
- Set up version control for documentation to track changes over time.
- Schedule regular reviews of the documentation (e.g., monthly) to ensure it stays current.

Continuous Re-Evaluation

However, as with most dynamic projects, needs may change over time. This brings us to the importance of continuous re-evaluation of these requirements. As more information emerges, whether through new research findings, user feedback, or shifts in market dynamics, revisiting and updating these data ensures that the ML system remains relevant and efficient.

Consider again the example of the recommendation engine. Initially, the focus might be on increasing sales through personalized suggestions. But after deployment, analytics might reveal that improving user retention is equally critical. Re-evaluating and adjusting the system's capabilities to meet this new goal could involve tweaking algorithms or incorporating additional data sources. This iterative process ensures that the system doesn't just meet its initial requirements but continues to deliver value over time.

Key Point: Regularly revisit and update requirements as new information emerges.

Example: Shifting focus from increasing sales to improving user retention based on post-deployment analytics.

Actionable Tips:

- Implement a formal change request process for updating requirements.

- Set up key performance indicators (KPIs) and monitor them regularly.

- Conduct retrospectives after each project milestone to gather insights and potential adjustments.

- Use A/B testing to validate assumptions and guide re-evaluation of features.

For software engineers aspiring to transition into ML roles, acknowledging these foundational aspects is quite important. They offer a systematic way to navigate the complexities of ML system design in interviews and real-world scenarios alike. Once you grasp the importance of recognizing explicit needs, engaging with stakeholders, documenting goals, and continuously re-evaluating necessities, you become better prepared to articulate their design choices and reasoning during interviews. Such proficiency is invaluable in showing readiness to tackle ML challenges effectively.

For data scientists and ML engineers preparing for technical interviews, these principles provide a solid foundation. They help structure thoughts and responses when faced with system design questions, which are often a significant part of interview processes at top tech companies. Mastery of these concepts boosts confidence and enhances your ability to address complex problems succinctly and comprehensively.

If you want to venture into careers in ML, familiarizing yourself with these industry-standard practices is essential. It demystifies the process of design, showing that it's about sophisticated algorithms as much as it is about thoughtful planning and strategic thinking. This knowledge prepares them for the kinds of discussions and problem-solving exercises they'll encounter in both academic and professional settings.

Practical Application in Interviews and Career Transitioon

For software engineers transitioning to ML roles or preparing for interviews:

1. Practice requirement gathering:
    - Use sample ML system design problems and write out detailed requirements.
    - Have peers review your requirements to ensure clarity and completeness.

2. Develop a personal checklist:
    - Create a go-to list of questions you'd ask to clarify requirements in any ML project.

3. Mock interviews:
    - Conduct mock interviews where you explain your process for requirement clarification.
    - Practice articulating trade-offs between different requirements.

4. Case study development:
    - Develop a case study showcasing how you applied these principles in a past project.
    - Highlight how your approach to requirements influenced the project's success.

5. Stay updated:
    - Follow ML blogs and case studies from top companies to understand industry best practices in requirement management.
    - Participate in ML forums or communities to discuss real-world challenges in requirement clarification.

Designing High-Level Architecture

Constructing a good high-level architecture for an ML system is very important in moving from concept to reality in ML design. When preparing for system design interviews, one key task is the selection of suitable models and algorithms. This choice depends significantly on the specifics of the problem you're addressing and the characteristics of your data. For instance, if you're dealing with a classification problem with labeled training data, supervised learning models like decision trees or support vector machines might be appropriate. On the flip side, unsupervised learning models such as K-means clustering could fit better when working with unlabeled data where patterns need to be identified.

Understanding Your Data

Understanding the nature of your data can guide your algorithm choice. Are you handling time-series data? Then consider recurrent neural networks (RNNs) that are adept at sequences. Is interpretability critical for your application? Decision trees or logistic regression might be preferable given their transparency. It's about using what fits—not just what's trendy.

Practical Exercise: Data Deep Dive

- Select a public dataset (e.g., from Kaggle).

- Spend 2 hours exploring the data:

    a. Generate summary statistics.

    b. Create visualizations (histograms, scatter plots, etc.).

    c. Identify potential issues (missing values, outliers, etc.).

    d. Propose preprocessing steps based on your findings.

Structuring Flow and Integration

Now, onto structuring data flow and integration. An ML system comprises multiple components, each with its own role in processing, storing, and integrating data. To allow seamless operation, defining how data flows between these components is important.

Practical Exercise: Pipeline Design Challenge

- Design a data pipeline for a real-time sentiment analysis system:

    a. Sketch the high-level architecture.

    b. List the components (e.g., data ingestion, preprocessing, model serving).

    c. Define the interfaces between components.

    d. Specify the technologies you'd use for each component (e.g., Kafka for streaming, TensorFlow Serving for model deployment).

User Interactions

Say you're building a recommendation system. Begin by designing how user interactions are captured and fed into feature extraction processes. You then need to outline how this data moves through the model training phase and ultimately informs recommendations delivered to users.

Practical Exercise: Recommendation System User Flow

- Design a recommendation system's user interaction and data flow:

a. Sketch the user interface for capturing interactions.

b. Map out how user data is collected and stored.

c. Design the feature extraction process from raw user data.

d. Outline the model training pipeline, including data preprocessing and model updating.

e. Plan how recommendations are generated and delivered back to users.

Using Pipelines for Flow Efficiency

You can use pipelines to structure this flow efficiently. Data pipelines automate the movement and transformation of raw data into meaningful insights, making sure consistency and reliability. Integration also needs tools and frameworks that support smooth interaction between modules, like Apache Kafka for handling real-time streaming data or batch-processing systems like Hadoop.

Practical Exercise: Pipeline Efficiency Workshop

- Choose a data-intensive ML task (e.g., large-scale image classification):

    a. Design a data pipeline covering data ingestion, preprocessing, feature extraction, and model training.

    b. Identify potential bottlenecks in your pipeline.

    c. Propose tools to address each stage (e.g., Apache Kafka for data ingestion, Apache Spark for distributed preprocessing).

    d. Outline a strategy for monitoring pipeline performance and identifying inefficiencies.

Modularity and Scalability

Considering modularity and scalability in design keeps your system futureproofed and flexible. Modularity means breaking down your system into independent modules that fulfill specific functions. This decoupling allows for easier updates and replacements without overhauling the entire system. Picture a fraud detection system: you might have separate modules for data ingestion, feature engineering, model scoring, etc. Each module functions independently yet cohesively within the larger framework.

Practical Exercise: Modular System Design

- Redesign an existing ML system for modularity:

    a. Break down the system into independent modules.

    b. Define clear interfaces for each module.

    c. Identify potential bottlenecks for scalability.

    d. Propose solutions to address these bottlenecks (e.g., using distributed computing, caching strategies).

Addressing Scalability and Edge Cases

Scalability is about ensuring your system can handle growth—be it more data, more users, or more complex operations.

Using Distributed Computing Solutions

Employ distributed computing solutions such as cloud services or Kubernetes to scale out your infrastructure. Serverless architectures can also help manage scaling as they automatically adjust resources based on demand. If you anticipate and design for growth, your solution can adapt gracefully to increased load and complexity, rather than buckle under pressure.

Practical Exercise: Scaling Strategy Design

- Design a scaling strategy for a high-traffic ML application:

    a. Estimate resource requirements for different levels of traffic.

    b. Choose between container orchestration (e.g., Kubernetes) and serverless architecture.

    c. Design an auto-scaling policy.

    d. Plan for data consistency and synchronization in a distributed environment.

    e. Outline a cost optimization strategy for cloud resources.

Implementing Failure Recovery Mechanisms

Another great aspect to take into account is implementing failure recovery mechanisms, which fortify your system's resilience. In any real-world setting, failures and unexpected issues are inevitable, whether due to hardware malfunctions, software bugs, or network disruptions. Designing with failure in mind means incorporating strategies that allow for quick recovery and minimal downtime.

Practical Exercise: Resilience Planning

- Design a failure recovery strategy for a critical ML system:

    a. Identify potential failure points.

    b. For each point, define:

    - Detection method
    - Alerting mechanism
    - Recovery procedure
    - Prevention strategy

    c. Implement a simple monitoring dashboard using tools like Prometheus and Grafana.

Employing Redundancy

One strategy is redundancy, where critical components are duplicated so that a backup is available should one fail. In addition, consider employing monitoring tools and alerting systems that detect anomalies early and notify engineers to intervene promptly. Automated rollback procedures can further minimize disruption by reverting to stable versions when new deployments encounter issues.

Practical Exercise: Resilience Planning Workshop

- Design a high-availability strategy for a critical ML system:

    a. Identify single points of failure in your architecture.

    b. Design redundancy for each critical component (e.g., database replication, load-balanced application servers).

    c. Implement a health check and an automated failover mechanism.

    d. Design a monitoring and alerting system to detect anomalies.

    e. Create an automated rollback procedure for model deployments.

    f. Develop a disaster recovery plan with defined Recovery Time Objective (RTO) and Recovery Point Objective (RPO).

Time Management and Common Mistakes During Interviews

Optimizing your interview performance is quite important when tackling ML system design problems. The key is to manage your time effectively, which starts with a thoughtful allocation of time across different phases of the interview. Let's say you have an hour: divide it wisely among requirement analysis, architecture design, and problem-solving. This strategic distribution ensures that each segment receives sufficient attention without the risk of rushing through critical parts. Let me give you an example. Say, you spend 15 minutes trying to understand the needs, 20 minutes sketching out an architecture, and leave the rest for developing and iterating on your solution. This way of doing things keeps you organized but also demonstrates to interviewers that you can handle complex tasks systematically.

Handling Pitfalls During Interviews

Moving on, it's very important to be aware of common pitfalls that many candidates fall into during interviews.

Over-Complicating: One frequent mistake is over-complicating solutions. It's tempting to showcase your knowledge, but simpler solutions often shine brighter by illustrating your ability to efficiently address the core problem.

Neglecting Edge Cases: Another oversight is neglecting edge cases, which can undermine the robustness of your solution. To combat this, always ask yourself what unusual inputs or scenarios might arise and how your system would handle them. Keeping these potential pitfalls in mind allows you to steer clear of traps that might otherwise sabotage your efforts.

Practice: As you know well by now, practice is another important piece when it comes to succeeding. Engaging in mock interviews can be incredibly beneficial. When you practice regularly, you'll find that your confidence grows alongside your competence.

Simulated interview scenarios provide a safe space to refine your articulation skills, improve your responsiveness to unexpected questions, and hone your overall presentation. Mock interviews are your playground to experiment with different angles and receive constructive feedback from peers or mentors. Embracing this practice makes actual interviews feel more familiar, reducing stress and enabling you to perform at your best.

Quizzes and Exercises

Quiz

1. What are the key steps in the systematic approach to ML system design problems presented in this chapter?

2. Why is clarifying requirements an essential first step in the problem-solving framework?

3. What types of questions should you ask to clarify the scope and constraints of a design problem?

4. In designing a high-level architecture, what are the main components you should consider for an ML system?

5. How do you address scalability concerns in your initial system design?

Mock Interview Problem

Problem Statement: Design a real-time recommendation system for a video streaming platform that suggests movies and TV shows to users based on their viewing history and preferences.

Instructions for the Interviewee: Apply the problem-solving framework discussed in this chapter to address this design challenge. Walk through each step, explaining your thought process and decisions. Remember to clarify requirements, design a high-level architecture, address scalability and edge cases, and manage your time effectively.

Key Insights and Practical Takeaways

- **Structured Approach:** Use a step-by-step method to tackle ML system design problems. Begin with decomposition, breaking large problems into manageable components. Prioritize functional requirements to focus on essential features first.

- **Iterative Enhancement:** Start with a simple solution and gradually increase complexity. This approach allows for quick testing, feedback, and continuous improvement of your design.

- **Systematic Evaluation:** Establish specific criteria for assessing each component of your ML system. Use metrics like accuracy, efficiency, and scalability to evaluate your design's effectiveness.

- **Clarifying Requirements:** Engage in effective stakeholder communication to understand explicit needs and constraints. Document goals and assumptions thoroughly, and continuously re-evaluate requirements as the project evolves.

- **High-Level Architecture:** Select appropriate models and algorithms based on the problem and data characteristics. Structure data flow and integration using pipelines and frameworks. Design for modularity and scalability to future-proof your system.

- **Interview Strategies:** Manage time effectively by allocating it wisely across different interview phases. Avoid common pitfalls like over-complicating solutions or neglecting edge cases. Practice with mock interviews and reflect on your performance to improve continuously.

CHAPTER 18

Case Studies and Practice Problems

Engaging with case studies and practice problems is a fantastic way to bridge theory and real-world application, especially in fields like ML and system design. These exercises are academic drills, as they reflect genuine complexities you might encounter when applying your knowledge to develop solutions for everyday challenges. When stepping into these scenarios, you can see firsthand how theoretical concepts play out in practice, giving you insights that are important for anyone venturing into the tech world.

Look at this chapter as a way for aspiring software engineers, data scientists, and students, where you'll get to the details of creating systems capable of handling e-commerce recommendations or detecting fraud. We'll explore detailed examples that mimic industry situations, allowing you to apply methods like collaborative filtering or anomaly detection in practical settings. When engaging with these examples, you'll gain a deeper knowledge of data handling, algorithm selection, and performance evaluation—skills that are key in technical interviews and real-world applications. Get ready to unravel complex scenarios with guided solutions, increasing your problem-solving toolkit and preparing you for the dynamic environment of ML and system design.

Detailed Case Study: E-commerce Recommendation System

When designing an e-commerce recommendation system, knowing user behavior is quite relevant for delivering personalized suggestions. Think of your favorite online store—how does it seem to know exactly what you're looking for?

Analyzing Behavior

Step-by-Step Process:

1. Define key user interactions to track (e.g., page visits, product views, purchases).

2. Implement tracking mechanisms (e.g., event logging).

3. Set up a data pipeline to collect and store user behavior data.

4. Perform exploratory data analysis (EDA) on collected data.

Hands-on Exercise: User Behavior Analysis

1. Use a sample e-commerce dataset (e.g., from Kaggle).

2. Perform the following analyses using Python and Pandas:

    - Calculate average time spent on product pages.

    - Identify most viewed and purchased product categories.

    - Analyze the correlation between page views and purchases.

3. Visualize your findings using Matplotlib or Seaborn.

Create Models

Once you analyze these behaviors, you can create models that predict which products a user might be interested in based on their past interactions. Say, if someone frequently buys sports equipment, a system could recommend the latest running shoes or gym accessories. The more data collected, the better the system becomes at customizing recommendations that feel almost intuitive.

Implementing Collaborative Filtering

Step-by-Step Process:

1. Choose between user-based or item-based collaborative filtering.

2. Prepare user-item interaction matrix.

3. Implement similarity computation (e.g., cosine similarity).

4. Generate recommendations based on similar users or items.

Hands-on Exercise: Simple Collaborative Filtering System

1. Implement a basic item-based collaborative filtering system.

2. Use the surprise library for easy implementation.

3. Evaluate the system using metrics like RMSE (Root Mean Square Error).

Adding ML

Step-by-Step Process:

1. Feature engineering from user and product data.

2. Choose suitable ML algorithms (e.g., decision trees, neural networks).

3. Train and validate models.

4. Implement a model serving real-time recommendations.

Hands-on Exercise: Decision Tree Recommender

1. Engineer features from user behavior and product data.

2. Implement a decision tree classifier for product recommendations.

3. Evaluate the a model using cross-validation.

A/B Testing

Step-by-Step Process:

1. Define metrics for measuring recommendation effectiveness.

2. Design A/B test (control group vs. treatment group).

3. Implement tracking for test groups.

4. Analyze results and make data-driven decisions.

Hands-on Exercise: Simple A/B Test

1. Simulate an A/B test for two recommendation algorithms.

2. Implement tracking for click-through rates (CTR).

3. Analyze the results using statistical tests.

Final Project: Build a Complete Recommendation System

Combine all the steps above to create a full-fledged recommendation system:

1. Set up a sample e-commerce dataset.
2. Implement user behavior tracking and analysis.
3. Develop a hybrid recommendation system using collaborative filtering and ML algorithms.
4. Design and implement an A/B testing framework.
5. Integrate privacy protection measures.
6. Create a simple web interface to demonstrate the recommendations.

Practice Problem: Real-Time Fraud Detection System

Let's now go through a practice problem to understand where your skills are at.

Acknowledging Fraudulent Patterns

Step-by-Step Process:

1. Collect historical transaction data (both fraudulent and legitimate).
2. Perform exploratory data analysis (EDA) to identify common fraud patterns.
3. Create visual representations of fraud patterns.
4. Develop a database of fraud indicators.

Hands-on Exercise: Fraud Pattern Analysis

1. Use a sample financial transaction dataset (e.g., from Kaggle).
2. Perform the following analyses using Python and Pandas:
    - Identify frequent small transactions within short time frames.
    - Analyze large sum transfers across multiple accounts.

- Visualize time patterns of fraudulent transactions.

Anomaly Detection Methods

Step-by-Step Process:

1. Choose appropriate anomaly detection algorithms (e.g., Isolation Forest, One-Class SVM).

2. Prepare data for anomaly detection (feature engineering).

3. Train and validate the anomaly detection model.

4. Set up real-time monitoring system for live transaction streams.

Hands-on Exercise: Anomaly Detection Implementation

1. Implement an Isolation Forest for anomaly detection.

2. Train the model on historical data.

3. Use the model to flag anomalies in a test dataset.

4. Evaluate the model's performance.

Supervised Learning Models

Step-by-Step Process:

1. Prepare a labeled dataset (fraudulent vs. legitimate transactions).

2. Perform feature engineering and selection.

3. Choose appropriate ML algorithms (e.g., Random Forest, XGBoost).

4. Train and validate models using cross-validation.

5. Implement a model serving real-time predictions.

Hands-on Exercise: Supervised Learning for Fraud Detection

1. Implement a Random Forest classifier for fraud detection.

2. Use feature importance to identify key fraud indicators.

3. Evaluate the model using cross-validation and ROC-AUC score.

Takeaways of Practice Problem Example

In practice, developing this kind of fraud detection system involves a series of real-world challenges. To give you an example, striking the right balance between sensitivity and specificity is essential. A system that's too sensitive may lead to numerous false alarms, overwhelming fraud analysts, and potentially frustrating customers with unnecessary verifications. On the other hand, a system with low sensitivity might miss significant fraud instances, leading to financial losses. Fine-tuning ML algorithms through iterative testing and validation is often needed to achieve optimal performance.

Quality and Quantity of Data

The quality and quantity of data are significant in how well these systems perform. Clean, well-labeled datasets improve the accuracy of supervised learning models. Although gathering such datasets can be challenging due to privacy concerns and the necessity for extensive collaboration across departments or even institutions, leveraging anonymized data and knowing how to comply with data protection regulations are significant considerations during system development.

Implementation of Fraud Detection System

Implementing an effective fraud detection system has also to do with integrating it seamlessly into existing IT infrastructure. Compatibility issues with legacy systems or third-party applications can hinder deployment unless addressed proactively. Designing modular components that can operate independently yet communicate effectively with each other can facilitate smoother integration processes and reduce disruptions to business operations.

Communication and Collaboration

Also, clear communication and collaboration between data scientists, engineers, and business stakeholders are instrumental in deploying an efficient fraud detection strategy. Data scientists bring expertise in model selection and evaluation, while engineers focus on system architecture and scalability. Business stakeholders provide insights into practical considerations and risk tolerance levels. Ensuring alignment among these groups throughout the development cycle can significantly improve outcomes.

Practice Problem: Large-Scale Image Classification Pipeline

As a software engineer transitioning to ML, an aspiring ML engineer preparing for interviews, or a computer science graduate aiming for a career in this field, understanding how to build and evaluate a scalable image classification pipeline is crucial. This guide will walk you through the key components and considerations.

Preprocessing

Effective data handling is the foundation of any image classification project. Preprocessing involves:

1. Cleaning the data.

2. Resizing images to a uniform scale.

3. Normalizing pixel values.

4. Applying image augmentation techniques (rotation, flipping, shifting).

These steps ensure data consistency and artificially expand your dataset, improving model robustness.

Convolutional Neural Networks

CNNs are the backbone of image classification tasks. They work as follows:

1. Breaking down visuals through multiple layers.

2. Identifying patterns and textures.

3. Progressively refining features from basic edges to complex objects.

For faster results, consider using pre-trained models like VGG-16 or ResNet50 with transfer learning.

Cloud-Based Deployment

Deploying at scale requires efficient use of cloud resources. Key considerations include:

1. AWS EC2 instances or Google's TensorFlow Extended (TFX) for distributed training.

2. Implementing parallel processing:

    o AWS: Use Amazon SageMaker for distributed training across multiple instances.

    o Google Cloud: Leverage AI Platform for scaling ML workloads.

3. Autoscaling:

    o AWS: Configure Auto Scaling groups to dynamically adjust EC2 instances.

    o Google Cloud: Use Kubernetes Engine's Cluster Autoscaler for automatic scaling.

Evaluating the Performance

Assess your model's performance using:

1. Cross-validation: Split the dataset into multiple folds for iterative training and validation.

2. Test datasets: Provide a final check before deployment.

3. Metrics: Accuracy, precision, recall, and F1 score.

Practical Implementation

When tackling a large-scale classification problem:

1. Segment your dataset (e.g., wildlife images into mammals, birds, reptiles).

2. Implement preprocessing for uniformity.

3. Choose an appropriate CNN architecture.

4. Deploy on a cloud platform with autoscaling configured.

Next Steps

To improve your image classification pipeline:

1. Regularly benchmark against industry standards.

2. Schedule periodic assessments during development.

3. Continuously integrate updated data and retrain your model.

4. Focus on optimizing cloud resource usage and cost-effectiveness.

5. Experiment with different CNN architectures and hyperparameters.

6. Stay updated on the latest advancements in image classification techniques.

Step-by-Step Solutions and Analysis

Providing Detailed Walkthroughs of Solving Complex Problems

Going on the path of solving complex problems, particularly in ML and system design, can often feel overwhelming. But by breaking down the problem scenario into manageable components, you can peel away the layers of complexity and tackle each part with clarity and precision. Imagine approaching a massive coding task as if you're dealing with a puzzle, where each piece represents an essential aspect of the problem at hand. Focusing on one component at a time allows you to simplify your workload and refine your method use towards a more efficient solution.

Break Into Pieces

So, when faced with designing a recommendation system, begin by fragmenting the broad challenge into smaller tasks: analyzing user behavior patterns, integrating various filtering techniques, and using appropriate algorithms. This segmentation allows for focused analysis and smoother transitions from one segment to another. Keep in mind that knowing how these individual segments interact is important, as it helps form the bigger picture of your solution strategy.

Action steps:

1. Identify the main components of the problem.
2. List each component separately.
3. Determine dependencies between components.

Example: Designing a recommendation system

- Components: User behavior analysis, Filtering techniques, Algorithm selection
- Dependencies: User behavior informs filtering, which affects algorithm choice

Apply Methodologies

Once you've segmented the problem, the next step is applying methodologies systematically at each stage of the solution. Think of it as following a recipe; however, instead of culinary delights, your end product is a well-designed system or solution. Begin by identifying which methods suit each component best. For example, statistical methods might be used for predictive analytics while neural networks could assist in pattern recognition. If you document each step meticulously, you make sure that everything progresses logically and nothing is left to guesswork. A popular methodology is Agile Development, where iterative cycles allow developers to adjust based on feedback. This adaptability is especially beneficial in fast-paced fields like ML.

For each component:

1. Define specific goals and requirements.

2. List potential methods or techniques to address it.

3. Evaluate pros and cons of each method.

Example: User behavior analysis

- Goal: Understand user preferences and patterns.

- Methods: a) Collaborative filtering b) Content-based filtering c) Hybrid approaches

- Evaluation: Compare accuracy, scalability, and data requirements

Applying Systematically:

1. Choose an appropriate methodology (e.g., Agile, Waterfall).

2. Break down the solution process into sprints or phases.

3. Set clear objectives for each sprint/phase.

4. Implement regular check-ins and reviews.

Example using Agile:

- Sprint 1: Develop basic user behavior analysis.

- Sprint 2: Implement initial filtering algorithm.

- Sprint 3: Integrate and test basic recommendation system.

- Sprint 4: Refine and optimize based on test results.

Add Guidelines

Consider incorporating guidelines at this stage, especially to highlight the importance of reviews and iterations. Revisiting previous steps to test assumptions and validate outcomes enhances accuracy and effectiveness. Developers should constantly ask themselves whether their current solutions align with the overarching problem goals and user requirements. Feedback loops are relevant during this phase, offering real-time insights that might dictate changes in approach.

1. Analyze test results and user feedback.

2. Identify areas for improvement.

3. Prioritize refinements based on impact and effort.

4. Implement changes in subsequent iterations.

Example: Refining recommendation algorithm

- Analyze user engagement with recommendations.

- Identify categories with low accuracy.

- Adjust algorithm weights or features for those categories.

- Retest and compare with previous results.

Look at Alternatives

Examining alternative angles gives valuable perspectives that may lead to even better solutions. It's important not to get tunnel vision regarding the initial approach taken. Alternative strategies might reveal efficiencies or innovative paths previously unseen. If a supervised learning model isn't yielding the desired results, consider switching to unsupervised or reinforcement learning techniques. When juxtaposing different models, you can compare strengths and weaknesses, ultimately finding the best solution. This examination doesn't just diversify your skill set but also makes you versatile in adapting solutions to fit diverse scenarios.

1. Research alternative solutions or emerging technologies.

2. Evaluate potential benefits and drawbacks.

3. Conduct small-scale experiments with promising alternatives.

4. Compare results with your current solution.

Example: Exploring deep learning for recommendations

- Research recent papers on deep learning in recommendation systems.

- Implement a small-scale neural network model.

- Compare performance with your current method.

- Decide whether to incorporate deep learning techniques.

Summarize Main Insights

Finally, summarizing the main insights gained from the process provides closure to the problem-solving path. This reflection allows an opportunity to assess what worked well and highlight areas for improvement. Sharing these insights promotes a culture of knowledge sharing within teams, allowing for collective growth and innovation. Often, these summaries are present in project retrospectives where teams review outcomes against initial objectives.

1. Maintain a detailed log of your problem-solving process.

2. Summarize key decisions and their rationales.

3. Document lessons learned and best practices.

4. Share findings with team members or the wider community.

Example: Documentation for a recommendation system project

- Create a project wiki outlining the system architecture.

- Write a technical blog post about overcoming scalability challenges.

- Present findings at a team knowledge-sharing session.

- Contribute insights to relevant online forums or conferences.

Design Challenges

Instructions: For each of the following design challenges, apply the problem-solving framework discussed in earlier chapters. Focus on clarifying requirements, designing high-level architecture, addressing scalability and edge cases, and considering real-world constraints. Spend about 30–45 minutes on each challenge.

Social Media Content Moderation System:

Design an ML-based content moderation system for a large social media platform that can automatically detect and flag inappropriate content (text, images, and videos) in real-time. Key considerations:

- Multi-modal input (text, image, video).

- Real-time processing requirements.

- Handling diverse types of inappropriate content.

- Balancing automation with human review.

- Scalability for millions of daily posts.

- **Predictive Maintenance for Industrial IoT:** Create a system that uses sensor data from industrial equipment to predict potential failures and schedule maintenance before breakdowns occur. Key considerations: Handling streaming data from multiple sensors.

- Dealing with imbalanced data (rare failure events).

- Incorporating domain knowledge into the ML model.

- Balancing prediction accuracy with false alarm rate.

- Integration with existing industrial systems.

- **Personalized News Aggregator:** Design a news recommendation system that aggregates articles from various sources and provides personalized recommendations to users based on their reading history, preferences, and current events. Key considerations:Real-time content ingestion and processing.

- Balancing personalization with diversity in recommendations.

- Handling cold start problem for new users.

- Incorporating trending topics and breaking news.

- Scalability for millions of articles and users.

- **Autonomous Vehicle Perception System:** Develop an ML system for an autonomous vehicle that can detect and classify objects in its environment, predict their movements, and make real-time decisions. Key considerations: Fusion of data from multiple sensors (cameras, LiDAR, radar).

- Real-time processing with strict latency requirements.

- Handling diverse environmental conditions (weather, lighting).

- Ensuring safety and reliability in critical situations.

- Continuous learning and model updates.

- **Large-Scale Language Model Serving System:** Design a system to serve a large language model (like GPT-3) that can handle various natural language processing tasks for multiple applications. Key considerations: Handling high-throughput, low-latency requests

- Managing computational resources efficiently

- Supporting multiple tasks (e.g., translation, summarization, question-answering)

- Versioning and updating the model

- Ensuring data privacy and security

- **Dynamic Pricing System for Ride-Sharing:** Create an ML system that dynamically adjusts prices for a ride-sharing service based on real-time demand, supply, and other relevant factors. Key considerations: Real-time data processing and decision making

- Balancing multiple objectives (maximizing revenue, rider satisfaction, driver utilization)

- Handling spatial and temporal variations in demand and supply

- Adapting to sudden changes (e.g., events, weather conditions)

- Ensuring fairness and transparency in pricing

For each challenge, consider the following steps:

1. Clarify the requirements and constraints.

2. Sketch a high-level system architecture.

3. Identify the main components and their interactions.

4. Discuss data flow and storage considerations.

5. Address scalability and performance issues.

6. Consider potential edge cases and how to handle them.

7. Discuss any ethical considerations or potential biases in the system.

After completing each design challenge, reflect on the following:

- What were the most challenging aspects of this design problem?

- How did you apply concepts from previous chapters to this challenge?

- What additional information or expertise would you need to refine this design further?

- How might this system evolve or need to adapt in the future?

Key Insights and Practical Takeaways

- **E-commerce Recommendation System:** Analyze user behavior patterns and implement collaborative filtering techniques. Use ML algorithms like decision trees or neural networks to process large datasets. Employ A/B testing to assess and improve system performance.

- **Real-time Fraud Detection System:** Identify common fraudulent patterns in transaction data. Apply anomaly detection methods to flag suspicious activities. Use supervised learning models trained on historical fraud data for prediction. Continuously update the system with new patterns to adapt to evolving fraud strategies.

- **Large-scale Image Classification Pipeline:** Implement effective preprocessing strategies for managing diverse image datasets. Utilize Convolutional Neural Networks (CNNs) for feature extraction and classification. Leverage cloud-based resources for distributed workload processing. Evaluate model performance using cross-validation and metrics like accuracy, precision, and recall.

- **Problem-Solving Approach:** Break down complex problems into manageable components. Apply methodologies systematically at each stage of the solution. Examine alternative approaches to find the best solution. Conduct thorough testing and iteration to evaluate effectiveness.

- **Design Challenges:** Practice applying the problem-solving framework to various ML system design scenarios. Focus on clarifying requirements, designing high-level architecture, addressing scalability, and considering real-world constraints.

CHAPTER 19

Advanced Interview Techniques

Mastering advanced interview techniques is essential for anyone getting into the ML space. Interviews can be more than just a test of technical ability; they are an opportunity to showcase a better understanding of both ethical and practical considerations that are important when designing intelligent systems. In this chapter, we dig into the often overlooked yet critical topic of ethics in ML system design. From tackling bias in algorithms to ensuring data privacy, knowing these ethical details is important to pass your interview and to build technology that positively impacts society.

Throughout this chapter, you'll know how to think about the ethical implications of your work from the ground up. We'll guide you through the process of acknowledging potential ethical pitfalls and integrating these insights right into the design phases of your projects. As you read on, expect to find practical strategies for balancing accuracy with fairness, knowing what trade-offs might mean for different stakeholders, and how you can articulate these considerations clearly during interviews. When exploring real-world examples and contemporary case studies, we'll give you the knowledge to approach your next ML interview with confidence and an ethical compass well-calibrated for the challenges ahead.

Handling Ambiguity and Incomplete Information

When stepping into the ML industry, interviews can be a daunting process. Add in the unpredictable nature of real-world data, and it's easy to feel overwhelmed. Although acknowledging uncertainty is the first step towards taming it. In any real-life scenario, data can be messy, incomplete, or ambiguous. These uncertainties shouldn't deter an engineer; rather, they should be seen as opportunities to show competence and adaptability. Recognizing uncertain data needs knowledge that perfection in datasets is rare. Instead, it's about managing these imperfections effectively to extract meaningful insights.

Asking Clarifying Questions

Next comes the simple but very important skill of asking clarifying questions during interviews. You're presented with a problem that seems straightforward but has hidden complexities lying beneath. This is where asking questions becomes significant. When you do this, you reveal assumptions that might not have been apparent at first glance. Suppose you're asked to design an algorithm for predicting weather patterns. On the surface, the task seems clear-cut, but probing further could uncover factors like seasonal variations, geographical nuances, or even data source reliability that aren't immediately obvious. Asking open-ended questions helps dig up missing information, laying a solid foundation for your approach.

Flexibility is another key player in managing uncertainty. Often, the best-laid plans need tweaking on the fly. Adaptive problem-solving is all about being open to change and thinking on your feet. Say you're halfway through implementing a ML model, and suddenly, the client wants to add new constraints. This is where flexibility shines. Instead of starting from scratch, assess what can be adjusted within the current framework to accommodate the changes. Practicing this skill during interviews will show your ability to adapt as well as highlight your readiness to embrace evolving challenges head-on.

Iterative Thinking

Iterative thinking is yet another powerful tool in your arsenal. It has to do with revisiting initial conclusions with new data and perspectives. Take, for instance, a situation where you've built a model based on certain assumptions. After running preliminary tests, you discover anomalies in the results. Rather than discarding the entire effort, iterative thinking encourages re-evaluation. Maybe additional data sets are needed, or perhaps tuning existing parameters could yield better performance. This cyclical process of hypothesizing, testing, and refining is invaluable in interviews, showing a methodical way to uncertainty—an essential trait for roles in ML.

Handling Ambiguity

To handle ambiguity and incomplete information efficiently, guidelines can be helpful.

Understand the Problem: The first thing you have to do is to make sure you clearly understand the scope of the problem. Misunderstandings often arise from vague instructions, so confirm details with your interviewer if needed.

Break Down the Issue: Once the scope is clear, break down the problem into manageable parts. When segmenting a large issue into smaller, more digestible components, you avoid feeling overwhelmed and can focus on solving one aspect at a time. Ensure that each segment is well-defined before proceeding to the next, minimizing the impact of uncertainty across the board.

Look at multiple Solutions: While discussing trade-offs or justifying decisions, remember to weigh multiple solutions. Balance pros and cons, and use evidence-based reasoning to support your choices. Even in interviews, articulating why one path was chosen over another reflects your ability to make informed decisions under pressure. It's about showing thoughtfulness and thoroughness in your way of operating—a skill highly valued in the tech industry.

Adopt Solutions According to Limitations: Lastly, adapt solutions according to different constraints by being resourceful. Consider the various limitations you might face, such as computational power or data availability. Simply by preparing adaptable strategies beforehand, you position yourself as a candidate ready for any challenge an interviewer might throw your way. Showing versatility with constraints highlights your capacity to address real-world obstacles—a must-have skill for a successful career in ML.

Discussing Trade-Offs and Justifying Decisions

Going through decision-making under constraints is an important skill for anyone stepping into ML system design. One of the first concepts to grasp in this environment is the idea of trade-offs. Trade-offs are unavoidable but integral, often arising when you must balance competing interests. Consider the classic tension between model accuracy and computational efficiency. While a highly accurate model might be more desirable, it could also require significant computing power, which isn't always feasible. Making informed decisions in these situations demands a clear understanding of which elements hold the most weight in your specific context.

Justifying Decisions

Articulating the justifications behind your decisions is another important component. This involves explaining what decision was made and why it was made. Effective articulation needs clarity and confidence. For example, if you're asked why a particular model architecture was chosen over another, it's not enough to say it seemed better. Instead, detail the reasons: perhaps one model had faster training times, or maybe it performed better with the specific data set you were working with. Practice expressing your rationale concisely, with a focus on the goals you prioritized. This skill becomes especially valuable during interviews, where showcasing your thought process can differentiate you from other candidates.

Evaluating Alternative Solutions Frameworks

Frameworks for evaluating alternative solutions provide structure when considering different paths you might take. Start with analyzing potential impacts—both positive and negative. A useful approach is to create a list of pros and cons for each solution, weighing them against your overarching objectives. Think about scalability, future maintenance, and how each option aligns with your long-term goals. Also, you can use case studies or historical examples where similar decisions have been faced and resolved effectively. This framework helps in visualizing outcomes before they happen, thereby minimizing risks associated with unforeseen consequences.

Ethical considerations are important in assessing the potential outcomes of decisions within ML projects. As algorithms increasingly influence main aspects of daily life, designers must be aware of the ethical implications tied to their choices. Questions such as whether a model perpetuates bias or infringes on user privacy are imperative. For instance, a healthcare AI application has to be examined meticulously to make sure it gives equitable service across diverse demographic groups. Ethical guidelines should not merely be an afterthought; instead, integrate them from the outset of the design process. Reference established ethical codes in technology to guide these discussions and maintain transparency in your assessments.

Consider incorporating whiteboarding and diagramming into your decision-making process, particularly during interviews. Visual representation increases knowledge and allows for immediate feedback and adaptation. Use diagrams to map out trade-offs or to compare potential impacts of different solutions side by side. This method allows for a tangible way for interviewers to follow your line of thinking, turning your decision-making process more accessible and compelling.

Adapting Solutions for Different Constraints

As a candidate preparing for technical interviews in this field, knowing how to adapt solutions to a variety of constraints is essential. Let's first go into the different types of constraints you may encounter—technical, budgetary, and temporal.

Addressing Technical Constraints

Technical constraints can include limitations on computational power, memory, or software capabilities. Just imagine for a moment you're working on a project where the end-user's device has low processing power. Your solution needs to function smoothly within these confines without degrading user experience. On the flip side, budgetary constraints often restrict access to high-end tools or expansive datasets.

Use Open-Source Public Datasets

A smart workaround might involve leveraging open-source technologies or public datasets to bridge the gap. Temporal limitations, such as tight deadlines, demand swift yet effective problem-solving skills. If you're coding a feature with a two-week timeframe, you might opt for an MVP (Minimum Viable Product) approach initially, just to know that the main functionalities are prioritized.

Redesign Your Solutions

Once you've grasped the nature of these constraints, the next step is redesigning your solutions to accommodate them. This doesn't just mean tweaking the current model but sometimes reinventing the wheel entirely. Consider the example of building an app intended to process large volumes of real-time data. If faced with budget constraints, instead of employing costly dedicated servers, a cloud-based service could be a more economical choice. In a similar way, rewriting algorithms to simplify computational requirements could help mitigate technical constraints.

Prioritizing elements of a solution amid these constraints can feel like a juggling act. However, establishing what's most critical is key. Start by breaking down the project goals and understanding which aspects align closely with these objectives. Say you're developing a facial recognition tool; accuracy and speed might take precedence over additional features like stylized overlays. Tools like the MoSCoW method (Must have, Should have, Could have, and Won't have) can also facilitate decision-making during prioritization.

Communicating Decisions

Communicating why you made certain decisions under constraints is an art in itself. Whether in an interview room or a team meeting, being able to articulate your thought process helps understanding and builds confidence in your solution. It helps to first lay out the constraint clearly. Was it a limited budget? A pressing deadline? Follow this by explaining how each element was addressed or adjusted. Using evidence from past projects can also bolster your explanation. If you streamlined a data pipeline to fit within a time limit, describing the specific steps you took and the impact they had makes your rationale tangible.

In interviews, clear communication isn't merely about stating facts but weaving a narrative around your choices. If you're asked how you'd handle scaling an algorithm under server limitations. Rather than simply listing steps, paint a picture:

> Given the server restrictions, I would prioritize refining the algorithm's efficiency. Initially, I'd analyze the heaviest processes using profiling tools, then re-engineer those to run asynchronously

where possible. This change aligns with the server's capacity and reduces overall processing time, improving user satisfaction.

Such storytelling captivates your audience and highlights your strategic thinking.

Effective Whiteboarding and Diagramming

Within the ML and system design space, being able to visualize your thoughts clearly is crucial. You may be well-versed in algorithms and data structures, but conveying complex concepts visually can often make or break your ability to communicate effectively. Say you're trying to explain how a neural network processes inputs without a clear diagram—it's almost impossible for the other person to fully grasp what you're saying. A well-structured illustration helps others understand your thought process and clarifies your own understanding. It's like turning a foggy idea into a coherent picture that everyone can see.

Best Practices in Creating Structured Diagrams

Now, let's talk about best practices in creating structured diagrams. Think of it as storyboarding your ideas before a big presentation. Using simple shapes—like circles for nodes and arrows for relationships—can significantly increase clarity. The goal is to make your diagram so intuitive that anyone looking at it can understand the basics with minimal explanation. Labeling is another main component; every element of your diagram should have a label that adds context to its purpose within the system. This method allows for your verbal explanations to be backed up by a visual counterpart that's easy to digest. Remember, a cluttered diagram can confuse, so maintain simplicity, focusing only on what's relevant for the concept you're presenting.

Importance of Iterative Diagramming

Next up is the importance of iterative diagramming. Nothing is perfect on the first try—diagramming is no different. Iteration allows you to capture changing thoughts and refine your visualizations based on immediate feedback. Just picture yourself in a whiteboarding session discussing a new ML model with peers. Your initial sketch might be basic, highlighting just the main components. As discussions progress, you're likely to receive input from others that enriches your original idea. When iterating on your diagram, you allow these new insights to shape and improve it. This ongoing refinement improves the quality of your presentation and promotes collaborative learning, opening the floor for diverse perspectives.

Whiteboards give you a unique advantage when it comes to highlighting main components and relationships. Unlike digital tools, they encourage an organic flow of ideas. You can quickly draw, erase, modify, and rearrange elements without the constraints often imposed by software. This flexibility is invaluable during brainstorming sessions where spontaneity can lead to groundbreaking insights. If you're mapping out a data pipeline, being able to easily switch between different configurations on a whiteboard can help identify potential bottlenecks or inefficiencies. It's an effective way to demonstrate connections between various parts of a system dynamically.

Guidelines aren't always necessary, but they can streamline your whiteboarding process if you feel overwhelmed. Start with a rough outline of the major sections you want to cover. Think of it as sketching a map before planning the route. A common strategy is to first draw the skeleton of your system—key inputs, outputs, and transformations—and then fill in the details. This method prevents you from getting lost in the weeds, and you know for sure that each part of your diagram has a distinct purpose. Consider annotating your drawings with brief notes explaining why certain decisions were made, providing further insight to those reviewing your work later.

Consider also the environment in which you're working. Lighting, board size, and available colors can all impact the effectiveness of your whiteboarding session. If you're in a room with limited resources, adapt by scaling down your diagrams to fit smaller spaces or using color strategically to differentiate elements. These situational adjustments allow your visual communication to remain impactful, regardless of external limitations.

Mock Interview Scenario

Interviewer: "Design an AI-powered hiring system for a large multinational corporation. The system should help streamline the hiring process, from resume screening to final candidate selection. Keep in mind the ethical implications and potential biases in such a system."

Candidate's Approach: (Clarify Requirements and Handle Ambiguity) Ask about the scale of hiring (number of applications, positions, departments); inquire about the specific stages of the hiring process to be included; clarify the level of human involvement desired in the process; ask about any specific regulatory or compliance requirements.

High-Level System Design (use whiteboard or digital tool): Draw a flowchart of the hiring process, including: Resume intake and parsing; Initial screening and ranking; Skills assessment; Interview scheduling and feedback collection; Final candidate ranking and selection; Highlight points where AI/ML models will be integrated; Indicate data flow and storage components.

Address Ethical Considerations: Discuss potential sources of bias (such as historical hiring data, resume language); Propose methods for ensuring fairness across different demographic groups; Suggest transparency measures for candidates; Address data privacy and security concerns.

Discuss Trade-offs: Automation vs. human oversight; Model complexity vs. interpretability; Efficiency vs. fairness; Personalization vs. standardization in the hiring process.

Discuss Key Components:

a. Data Ingestion and Preprocessing

- Resume parsing and feature extraction
- Standardization of job descriptions and requirements

b. ML Models

- Resume ranking model
- Skills assessment model
- Interview performance prediction model

c. Bias Detection and Mitigation Module

- Continuous monitoring of model outputs for bias.
- Techniques for reducing bias (e.g., adversarial debiasing, reweighting).

d. Explainability Layer

- Providing reasoning for model decisions.
- Generating reports for hiring managers and candidates.

Adapt to Different Constraints:

Interviewer: "How would your design change if this system needed to work across different countries with varying labor laws and data protection regulations?" Candidate: Discuss adaptations such as:

- Modular design to accommodate different regulatory requirements.

- Localized data storage and processing.
- Customizable bias detection based on country-specific protected attributes.
- Flexible reporting and explainability features.

Scalability and Performance:
- Discuss strategies for handling high volume of applications during peak hiring seasons.
- Propose caching and load balancing techniques for real-time components (e.g., skills assessments).

Monitoring and Improvement:
- Suggest metrics for tracking system performance and fairness.
- Propose a feedback loop for continuous improvement of ML models.
- Discuss the importance of regular audits and third-party evaluations.

Throughout the interview, the candidate should:
- Clearly explain their thinking process.
- Use the whiteboard/diagramming tool effectively to illustrate complex ideas.
- Ask clarifying questions when faced with ambiguity.
- Proactively discuss ethical implications and potential biases.
- Be prepared to adapt their design based on the interviewer's feedback or additional constraints.

Interviewer's Potential Follow-Up Questions:
1. How would you ensure that the system doesn't inadvertently discriminate against protected groups?
2. Can you elaborate on how the explainability layer would work for complex ML models?
3. What kind of data would you need to train these models, and how would you ensure their quality and representativeness?

4. How would you handle a situation where the AI system's recommendation conflicts with a human recruiter's opinion?

5. What metrics would you use to evaluate the success of this system beyond just hiring efficiency?

This mock interview scenario challenges the candidate to not only design a complex ML system but also to critically consider its ethical implications and real-world constraints. It provides opportunities to demonstrate advanced interview techniques such as handling ambiguity, discussing trade-offs, and adapting to new constraints.

Key Insights and Practical Takeaways

- **Handling Ambiguity:** Incomplete data is a common challenge. Use clarifying questions to uncover hidden complexities in interviews, demonstrating your problem-solving skills.

- **Flexibility in Solutions:** Adapt your approach when new constraints arise. Iterative thinking and flexibility in execution highlight your ability to handle evolving requirements.

- **Balancing Trade-offs:** Be prepared to explain trade-offs, such as balancing accuracy and computational efficiency, and justify your decisions with clear reasoning during interviews.

- **Ethical Awareness:** Incorporate ethics into your design process. Addressing issues like bias and fairness shows awareness of the broader implications of your work.

- **Adapting to Constraints:** Showcase how you can adapt solutions to technical, budgetary, or time constraints by focusing on priorities and using available resources effectively.

- **Visual Communication:** Use diagrams and whiteboarding to make complex ideas clear and easy to follow during interviews. Visual aids help convey your thought process.

CHAPTER 20

Final Preparation and Future Trends

Preparing for the future of ML is all about understanding how emerging trends shape system design and making sure you're ready to grow with the field. ML isn't just about building algorithms; it's also about creating systems that can adapt, process efficiently, and meet the demands of a changing tech landscape. When stepping into the ML space, it's important to grasp the theoretical aspects as well as the real-world applications that drive innovation.

Here, we'll explore the main principles of ML system design, going into concepts like simplicity and modularity which are relevant in building great systems. Looking at how scalable architectures and efficient frameworks allow your ML models to handle growing data demands is also something that we will talk about. We'll also tackle common challenges such as overfitting and data quality issues, giving you strategies to mitigate these issues. Evaluating performance using various metrics beyond mere accuracy—like precision and recall—can give you a rounded view of your model's success, too. We'll end with tips for creating a comprehensive cheat sheet, perfect for technical interviews, while guiding you through strategic interview preparation techniques so you're ready to showcase your skills in any scenario.

Comprehensive ML System Design Cheat Sheet

ML System Design Cheat Sheet

1. Key Principles:

    a. Simplicity: Keep designs straightforward for better understanding and maintenance.

    b. Modularity: Break systems into manageable components for flexibility and scalability.

c. Scalability: Design to handle increased loads smoothly.

   d. Efficiency: Optimize algorithms and data processing to minimize resource use.

2. Architecture Components:

   e. Data Collection & Preprocessing

   f. Feature Engineering • Model Selection & Training

   g. Evaluation & Validation

   h. Deployment & Monitoring

3. Scalability Strategies:

   i. Horizontal scaling (adding more machines)

   j. Vertical scaling (upgrading existing machines)

   k. Distributed computing frameworks (e.g., Apache Spark)

   l. Cloud-based solutions (AWS, Google Cloud, Azure)

4. Common Pitfalls:

   m. Overfitting: Use regularization, cross-validation

   n. Data quality issues: Implement robust preprocessing

   o. Concept drift: Continuous monitoring and retraining

   p. Scalability bottlenecks: Profile and optimize critical paths

5. Performance Metrics:

   q. Accuracy, Precision, Recall, F1-score

   r. ROC curve and AUC • Mean Squared Error (MSE) for regression

   s. Confusion matrix for classification

6. Model Selection Guidelines:

t. Linear models: Simple, interpretable, for linearly separable data

   u. Tree-based models: Handle non-linear relationships, good for tabular data

   v. Neural Networks: Complex patterns, large datasets, image/text data

   w. Ensemble methods: Combine multiple models for better performance

7. Deployment Considerations:

   x. Containerization (e.g., Docker) for consistency

   y. CI/CD pipelines for smooth updates

   z. A/B testing for gradual rollout

   aa. Monitoring and logging for system health

8. Error Handling Strategies:

   bb. Graceful degradation

   cc. Fallback mechanisms

   dd. Automated alerts and notifications

   ee. Regular backups and recovery plans

9. Optimization Techniques:

   ff. Feature selection and dimensionality reduction

   gg. Hyperparameter tuning (e.g., grid search, random search)

   hh. Model compression for deployment

   ii. Caching and data indexing for faster retrieval

10. Ethical Considerations:

    jj. Bias detection and mitigation

    kk. Data privacy and security measures

ll. Interpretability and explainability of models

mm. Compliance with relevant regulations (e.g., GDPR)

Top 10 ML System Design Interview Questions and Approaches

1. Design a recommendation system for an e-commerce platform.

2. Create a real-time fraud detection system for a financial institution.

3. Develop an image classification system that can handle millions of images daily.

4. Design a chatbot that can understand and respond to customer queries.

5. Build a system for predictive maintenance in an industrial setting.

6. Create a content moderation system for a social media platform.

7. Design a system for autonomous vehicle navigation.

8. Develop a personalized news feed algorithm.

9. Create a large-scale language translation system.

10. Design a real-time bidding system for online advertising.

Strategies for Tackling These Questions:

1. Use the STAR Technique:

    a. Situation: Describe the context

    b. Task: Define the problem clearly

    c. Action: Explain your approach

    d. Result: Discuss expected outcomes

2. Highlight Key Components:

    a. Data ingestion and preprocessing

    b. Feature engineering

      c. Model selection and training

      d. Evaluation metrics

      e. Deployment and monitoring

3. Address Scalability:

      a. Discuss distributed computing solutions

      b. Mention cloud-based architectures

      c. Explain data partitioning strategies

4. Showcase Adaptability:

      a. Propose solutions for limited resources

      b. Discuss handling missing or noisy data

      c. Mention techniques for cold start problems

5. Demonstrate Creativity:

      a. Suggest innovative data collection methods

      b. Propose unique feature engineering ideas

      c. Discuss combining multiple models or techniques

6. Consider Ethical Implications:

      a. Address potential biases in data or models

      b. Discuss privacy concerns and data protection

      c. Mention model interpretability when relevant

7. Highlight Trade-offs:

      a. Discuss accuracy vs. computational efficiency

      b. Explain batch vs. real-time processing choices

      c. Mention model complexity vs. interpretability

8. Use Real-world Examples:

      a. Reference similar systems in industry

      b. Discuss potential challenges based on case studies

      c. Relate your experience to the problem at hand

9. Address Edge Cases:

      a. Discuss handling rare events or outliers

      b. Mention strategies for dealing with system failures

      c. Explain approaches for handling unexpected inputs

10. Conclude with Evaluation and Iteration:

      a. Discuss relevant performance metrics

      b. Explain A/B testing strategies

      c. Mention continuous learning and model updating

Mock Interview With Full Analysis and Feedback

Securing a role in ML often hinges on the ability to excel in interviews. One effective way to prepare for such crucial interactions is by engaging in mock interviews, which replicate real-life scenarios you might encounter. Once you immerse yourself in these practice sessions, you can familiarize yourself with the dynamics of technical interviews if you're either tackling complex system design problems or articulating your approach to ML applications.

Mock interviews are invaluable because they allow you to simulate the pressure and challenges of actual interviews without the stakes being as high. These practice sessions can be customized to cover a range of questions, from explaining a model's architecture to detailing an algorithm's efficiency. As you rehearse these responses, focus on clarity and relevance. This thorough practice helps in honing your ability to think on your feet and provides insight into different styles of questioning you may encounter.

Detailed Analysis

An important aspect of these mock interviews is the detailed analysis of how you construct and deliver your responses. It's all about finding that sweet spot between technical depth and concise communication. Consider, for example, how you might explain a concept like overfitting. You'll need to show your understanding by discussing its causes, implications, and possible solutions, all while allowing your explanation to be clear and not overly verbose. Being mindful of this balance shows your grasp of the subject and reflects your ability to articulate complex ideas effectively—a skill highly valued in employers.

Feedback

Feedback is another foundation for refining your interview performance. Constructive feedback identifies both your strengths and areas needing improvement. Perhaps your explanations are great, yet your delivery lacks confidence, or maybe you have a tendency to go too deep into specifics at the expense of the bigger picture. Feedback sheds light on these patterns and provides actionable insights into how you can adjust and increase your technique. It might come from peers, mentors, or even self-assessment through recorded sessions. The goal is to build a comprehensive understanding of what you do well and what needs further development.

It's very important to add this feedback into subsequent rounds. You start understanding recurrent themes or problematic phrases in your responses. If you frequently resort to filler words, consciously replacing them with pauses can improve your speech quality and demonstrate thoughtfulness. Addressing these incrementally boosts your overall presentation and increases your readiness for the real interview.

Confidence

Confidence, as they say, is half the battle won. Developing this trait is integral to the preparation process and translates directly into your communication skills. Techniques such as the "power pose" or visualizing success can positively influence your mindset. Before an interview, taking a moment to engage in deep breathing exercises can help calm nerves and center your thoughts. Emphasizing the positive aspects of past performances also reinforces a confident outlook.

Another method to cultivate confidence is through storytelling. Contextualizing your experiences or illustrating concepts with anecdotes makes your dialogue more relatable and memorable. Imagine explaining a project where you implemented a novel ML solution; outlining it as a narrative can captivate your listener and make your technical prowess shine.

Communication

Effective communication is multifaceted, encompassing not only what you say but also how you say it. It involves everything from maintaining a steady pace of speech to employing appropriate body language. Engaging in regular reflection on these elements hones your ability to project assurance and competence. Also, practicing active listening allows you to address the interviewer's queries precisely rather than veering off-course, which shows respect and attentiveness.

Practicing under conditions simulating real-world interviews allows for an invaluable experience, allowing you to refine the technical substance of your answers as well as the manner in which you convey them. Such preparation builds the capability to confidently and effectively handle the diverse scenarios likely to unfold in a ML interview setting.

Mock Interview Scenario: ML System Design

Interviewer: "Design a real-time recommendation system for a video streaming platform."

Candidate: "Thank you for the question. Before I start, may I ask a few clarifying questions?"

Interviewer: "Certainly, go ahead."

Candidate: "What's the scale of the platform? How many users and videos are we dealing with?"

Interviewer: "Let's say we have about 50 million active users and a library of 100,000 videos."

Candidate: "Great, thank you. I'll outline my approach using the STAR method."

Situation: We need to design a real-time recommendation system for a video streaming platform with 50 million active users and 100,000 videos.

Task: Create a system that provides personalized video recommendations to users in real-time, improving user engagement and watch time.

Action:

1. Data Collection:

    - User data: viewing history, ratings, watch time

- Video data: genre, length, cast, release date
- Interaction data: clicks, pauses, fast-forwards

2. Feature Engineering:
    - User features: genre preferences, viewing patterns
    - Video features: popularity, average rating
    - Contextual features: time of day, device type

3. Model Selection:
    - Collaborative Filtering for user-item interactions
    - Content-Based Filtering for video similarities
    - Hybrid approach combining both methods

4. Real-time Processing:
    - Use Apache Kafka for real-time data streaming
    - Implement online learning for model updates

5. Scalability:
    - Distribute computation using Apache Spark
    - Use microservices architecture for flexibility

6. Evaluation:
    - Metrics: click-through rate, watch time, user satisfaction
    - A/B testing for comparing model versions

Result: This system should provide personalized, real-time recommendations, improving user engagement and watch time. We'll continuously monitor performance and iterate based on user feedback and metrics.

Interviewer: "That's a good overview. Can you elaborate on how you'd handle the cold start problem for new users or videos?"

Candidate: "Certainly. For new users, we could..."

[The interview continues with more specific questions and answers]

Analysis and Feedback:

Strengths:

1. Used STAR method effectively

2. Asked clarifying questions before starting

3. Provided a structured approach to the problem

4. Addressed key components: data, model, scalability, evaluation

Areas for Improvement:

1. Could provide more specific details on model architecture.

2. Didn't discuss potential challenges or limitations.

3. Might elaborate more on the real-time aspect of recommendations.

Next Steps for Practice:

1. Research and prepare for common follow-up questions.

2. Practice explaining technical concepts more concisely.

3. Develop examples of handling trade-offs in system design.

Strategies to Develop Your Goals

Let's now get into the strategies for setting and achieving personal development goals, making sure they align with your career aspirations. Start by conducting a self-assessment to highlight your strengths and areas that need improvement. Setting SMART (Specific, Measurable, Achievable, Relevant, Time-bound) goals can really help in crafting a clear path forward. If you want to master TensorFlow, set specific milestones, such as completing an intermediate online course within three months, followed by building a mini-project to demonstrate your skills.

Goals also need regular review and adjustment. As you achieve certain targets, reassess your objectives in light of changing industry needs or personal interests. Employing tools like productivity apps or digital planners can streamline goal tracking and promote accountability. Sharing your goals with mentors or colleagues can further boost motivation and offer external perspectives on your progress.

Embracing lifelong learning is another aspect of maintaining competitiveness in the ML field. Given how rapidly technology evolves, adopting a mindset of continuous education ensures you're always ready for the next big shift. Whether through formal education like advanced degrees or certifications or informal avenues like blogs, webinars, and MOOCs (Massive Open Online Courses), there's no shortage of learning resources available.

Importantly, lifelong learning shouldn't be confined to technical skills alone. Soft skills like communication, teamwork, and leadership are equally relevant, particularly when transitioning to roles involving ML system design. Improving these abilities can improve collaboration with multidisciplinary teams, promoting smoother integration of systems across different areas of a business.

Finally, implement a personal learning schedule to allow regular skill enhancement. Allocate time weekly for catching up on industry trends, experimenting with new coding techniques, or even revisiting foundational concepts that underpin more advanced theories. The consistency of small, regular learning sessions often yields better retention and understanding compared to sporadic cramming of information.

Final Preparation Checklist

Use this checklist in the days leading up to your ML system design interview to ensure you're fully prepared.

Technical Review

- Review core ML algorithms and their applications
- Supervised learning: regression, classification
- Unsupervised learning: clustering, dimensionality reduction
- Deep learning: CNNs, RNNs, Transformers

- Brush up on key ML concepts

- Evaluation metrics

- Bias-variance tradeoff

- Overfitting and underfitting

- Revisit system design fundamentals

- Scalability principles

- Load balancing

- Caching strategies

- Database choices (SQL vs. NoSQL)

- Review ML-specific system components

- Data pipelines

- Feature stores

- Model serving architectures

- Refresh knowledge on cloud services relevant to ML (like AWS SageMaker, Google Cloud AI Platform)

Practical Preparation

- Practice whiteboarding/diagramming ML system architectures.

- Solve at least 5 ML system design problems from end to end.

- Conduct 2–3 mock interviews with peers or mentors.

- Record yourself explaining a system design and review for areas of improvement.

- Create a list of clarifying questions for common design scenarios.

- Prepare 2–3 real-world examples of ML systems you've worked on or studied in depth.

Interview Strategy

- Review the problem-solving framework discussed in Chapter 17.
- Practice time management for different interview durations (30, 45, 60 minutes).
- Prepare a structured approach for discussing trade-offs in system design.
- Review techniques for handling ambiguity and incomplete information.
- Practice adapting your solutions to different constraints or requirements.

Company-Specific Preparation

- Research the company's ML products and services.
- Understand the company's technical stack and preferred technologies.
- Read recent technical blog posts or papers from the company.
- Prepare thoughtful questions about the company's ML initiatives.

Soft-Skills

- Practice articulating complex ideas clearly and concisely.
- Prepare for behavioral questions related to teamwork and problem-solving.
- Review techniques for active listening and effective communication.

Final Logistics

- Confirm interview details (time, location/link, interviewer names if provided).
- For on-site interviews: Plan your route and aim to arrive 15 minutes early.
- For virtual interviews: Test your internet connection, camera, and microphone.
- Prepare your interview space (quiet, well-lit, professional background).
- Gather necessary materials (resume copies, notepad, pen, water).

Ethical Considerations

- Review common ethical issues in ML (bias, fairness, privacy).

- Prepare examples of how to address ethical concerns in system design.

- Familiarize yourself with relevant regulations (e.g., GDPR, CCPA).

Day Before the Interview

- Review the ML System Design Cheat Sheet from this chapter.

- Go through one last practice problem.

- Prepare and lay out your outfit.

- Get a good night's sleep.

Morning of the Interview

- Eat a healthy breakfast

- Review your strongest examples and key talking points.

- Do some light exercise or stretching to reduce stress.

- Arrive early or log in to the virtual interview platform with time to spare.

Post-Interview

- Plan to send a thank-you email within 24 hours.

- Reflect on the interview experience and note areas for improvement.

- Regardless of the outcome, consider how you can use this experience for growth.

Key Insights and Practical Takeaways

- **ML System Design Principles:** Focus on simplicity and modularity in design. Integrate scalable and efficient architectures, leveraging cloud-based solutions for flexibility. Address common challenges like overfitting and data quality issues.

- **Performance Evaluation:** Look beyond accuracy to metrics like precision, recall, and F1-score. Use ROC curves and AUC values for a holistic view. Implement continuous monitoring and re-assessment to adapt to changing conditions.

- **Interview Preparation:** Develop a comprehensive cheat sheet summarizing key ML system design principles. Practice answering the top 10 ML system design interview questions using structured approaches like the STAR technique.

- **Mock Interviews:** Engage in mock interviews with detailed analysis and feedback. Focus on balancing technical depth with clear communication. Incorporate constructive feedback to improve performance in subsequent practice sessions.

- **Continuous Learning:** Stay updated with industry trends through reputable online platforms, newsletters, and podcasts. Join professional communities and participate in hackathons to expand your network and problem-solving skills.

Conclusion

As we end this path through ML system design, let's take a moment to talk about what we've explored together and how it can propel you into your future roles and interviews. Our exploration has taken us through the critical concepts and tools needed to bridge the gap between understanding traditional programming and stepping into ML.

First off, think about the main ideas we've covered: understanding the architecture of ML systems, the importance of scalability, data flow, latency considerations, and how to tackle complex problems by breaking them down into digestible parts. By now, these terms and principles shouldn't feel like buzzwords anymore; they should resonate with you as important components in mastering system design for ML applications. Knowing how to code is not enough anymore. Now, it's about thinking beyond the lines of code—embracing the interplay between data and algorithms to create solid, scalable solutions that stand up under the pressures of real-world use cases.

No matter which audience you fall into, these concepts form the foundation of everything you'll do going forward. They are essential for cracking interviews and for thriving in the dynamic world that is modern technology. We've mentioned practical insights throughout the chapters to make sure you understand but also that you know how to apply these principles effectively. Real-world practice will be your best teacher. Whether it's embarking on side projects, contributing to open-source initiatives, or replicating industry case studies, put yourself out there. Experimentation, after all, fuels innovation. As you test these waters, you'll notice your confidence grow. You'll see improvements in how you articulate complex ideas and make informed decisions. This transition isn't just professional—it's personal growth too.

Looking ahead, it's essential to keep an eye on the horizon. ML isn't stagnant; it's always changing with trends that often redefine industries. From advancements in neural network architectures to breakthroughs in unsupervised learning and federated learning, staying updated with new technologies will place you at the forefront of innovation. Consider keeping tabs on research papers, industry podcasts, and ML communities. The goal here isn't just to prepare for what's current but to anticipate and adapt to what's next. This proactive approach will set you apart from others who may rest on their laurels with yesterday's knowledge.

We live in a time where ethical considerations in AI and ML aren't just conversations—they're actionable imperatives. Think about bias reduction, privacy preservation, and developing models that reflect fairness and equity. These are technical challenges but also moral ones, and tackling them head-on will align your work with today's societal values and contribute to making technology inclusive and beneficial for everyone.

Ultimately, remember that preparation is only one part of the equation. Just as important is the mindset with which you approach both your career and your interviews. Believe in your ability to learn and grow. Embrace failures as opportunities to refine your understanding. Building confidence takes time—especially in today's technology space—but it's imperative. A positive outlook combined with a willingness to persist is powerful. It's what turns potential setbacks into setups for comebacks.

You have to keep in mind that even the most experienced professionals started exactly where you are now. Lean into your curiosity, promote resilience, and nurture the hunger to continuously improve. In doing so, you'll transform your skillset and perspectives.

So whether you're contemplating a thrilling leap into a new role, wanting to ace that dream interview, or feeding an academic passion for ML, I hope this book is both a guide and a companion. While this chapter closes, your story is far from over. Embrace what comes next with enthusiasm and determination.

In closing, thank you for allowing me to be part of your learning experience. Here's to the successes you'll achieve, the innovations you'll lead, and the futures you'll forge. Keep advancing—your contributions in the field of ML await!

Oh, and before I go, if you want a more general idea of system design interviews or to improve your knowledge on the subject, have a look at the other book in the series called "System Design Interview."

Glossary

- **A/B Testing:** A method of comparing two versions of a system or model to determine which performs better.

- **Accuracy:** The proportion of correct predictions (both true positives and true negatives) among the total number of cases examined.

- **Algorithm:** A step-by-step procedure or formula for solving a problem or accomplishing a task.

- **Anomaly Detection:** The identification of rare items, events, or observations that differ significantly from the majority of the data.

- **API (Application Programming Interface):** A set of protocols and tools for building software applications.

- **Batch Processing:** A method of processing data in large groups, typically used for tasks that don't require real-time results.

- **Bias:** A systematic error introduced into sampling or testing by selecting or encouraging one outcome or answer over others.

- **Big Data:** Extremely large data sets that may be analyzed computationally to reveal patterns, trends, and associations.

- **Classification:** A supervised learning task where the output variable is a category or class.

- **Collaborative Filtering:** A method of making automatic predictions about the interests of a user by collecting preferences from many users.

- **Confusion Matrix:** A table used to describe the performance of a classification model on a set of test data for which the true values are known.

- **Continuous Integration/Continuous Deployment (CI/CD):** The practice of automating the integration of code changes and the deployment of new versions.

- **Cross-Validation:** A model validation technique for assessing how the results of a statistical analysis will generalize to an independent data set.

- **Data Augmentation:** Techniques used to increase the amount of data by adding slightly modified copies of already existing data or newly created synthetic data.

- **Data Drift:** The change in model input data that leads to model performance degradation over time.

- **Data Pipeline:** A series of data processing steps, typically including data extraction, transformation, and loading (ETL).

- **Data Warehouse:** A system used for reporting and data analysis, considered a core component of business intelligence.

- **Deep Learning:** A subset of machine learning that uses multi-layered neural networks to learn from data.

- **Dimensionality Reduction:** The process of reducing the number of random variables under consideration by obtaining a set of principal variables.

- **Distributed Computing:** A model in which components of a software system are shared among multiple computers to improve efficiency and performance.

- **Ensemble Learning:** A machine learning paradigm where multiple models are used to solve a particular problem.

- **ETL (Extract, Transform, Load):** A process in database usage and data warehousing that involves extracting data from various sources, transforming it to fit operational needs, and loading it into the end target database.

- **Evaluation Metric:** A measure used to assess the performance of a machine learning model.

- **Feature Engineering:** The process of using domain knowledge to extract features from raw data via data mining techniques.

- **Feature Selection:** The process of selecting a subset of relevant features for use in model construction.

- **Federated Learning:** A machine learning technique that trains an algorithm across multiple decentralized edge devices or servers holding local data samples, without exchanging them.

- **Gradient Descent:** An optimization algorithm used to minimize some function by iteratively moving in the direction of steepest descent.

- **Grid Search:** A method of hyperparameter tuning that will methodically build and evaluate a model for each combination of algorithm parameters specified in a grid.

- **Hyperparameter:** A parameter whose value is set before the learning process begins, as opposed to parameters which are learned during training.

- **Hyperparameter Tuning:** The process of choosing a set of optimal hyperparameters for a learning algorithm.

- **Inference:** The process of using a trained machine learning model to make predictions.

- **K-Fold Cross-Validation:** A resampling procedure used to evaluate machine learning models on a limited data sample.

- **Kubernetes:** An open-source container-orchestration system for automating application deployment, scaling, and management.

- **Latency:** The time delay between the cause and the effect of some physical change in the system being observed.

- **Load Balancing:** The process of distributing network or application traffic across multiple servers.

- **Machine Learning Pipeline:** An end-to-end construct that orchestrates the flow of data into and out of a machine learning model or set of models.

- **Microservices:** An architectural style that structures an application as a collection of loosely coupled services.

- **Model Drift:** The decay of a model's prediction power as a result of changes in the environment and the relationships between input and output variables.

- **Model Serving:** The process of taking a trained machine learning model and making it available to serve predictions.

- **Natural Language Processing (NLP):** A field of artificial intelligence concerned with the interactions between computers and human language.

- **Overfitting:** A modeling error that occurs when a function is too closely fit to a limited set of data points.

- **Precision:** The ratio of correctly predicted positive observations to the total predicted positive observations.

- **Principal Component Analysis (PCA):** A statistical procedure that uses an orthogonal transformation to convert a set of observations of possibly correlated variables into a set of values of linearly uncorrelated variables.

- **Quantization:** The process of constraining an input from a continuous or otherwise large set of values to a discrete set.

- **Random Forest:** An ensemble learning method for classification, regression, and other tasks that operates by constructing a multitude of decision trees.

- **Recall:** The ratio of correctly predicted positive observations to all observations in actual class.

- **Recommender System:** A subclass of information filtering system that seeks to predict the "rating" or "preference" a user would give to an item.

- **Regression:** A set of statistical processes for estimating the relationships between a dependent variable and one or more independent variables.

- **Reinforcement Learning:** An area of machine learning concerned with how software agents ought to take actions in an environment so as to maximize some notion of cumulative reward.

- **Scalability:** The capability of a system, network, or process to handle a growing amount of work, or its potential to be enlarged to accommodate that growth.

- **Serverless Computing:** A cloud computing execution model in which the cloud provider runs the server and dynamically manages the allocation of machine resources.

- **Streaming:** The process of delivering or obtaining data (particularly audio or video) over a computer network as a steady, continuous flow.

- **Supervised Learning:** A type of machine learning where the algorithm learns on a labeled dataset.

- **TensorFlow:** An open-source software library for dataflow and differentiable programming across a range of tasks.

- **Transfer Learning:** A machine learning method where a model developed for a task is reused as the starting point for a model on a second task.

- **Underfitting:** A modeling error that occurs when a function is too simple to capture the underlying structure of the data.

- **Unsupervised Learning:** A type of machine learning that looks for previously undetected patterns in a data set with no pre-existing labels and with minimal human supervision.

- **Validation Set:** A set of data used to tune hyperparameters and assess model fit during training, with the aim of preventing overfitting.

- **Version Control:** A system that records changes to a file or set of files over time so that you can recall specific versions later.

References

Ajitsaria, A. (2019, July 10). *Build a Recommendation Engine with Collaborative Filtering*. Real Python. https://realpython.com/build-recommendation-engine-collaborative-filtering/

Amankwah, K. (2023, April 22). *MLOps: Best Practices for Deploying Machine Learning Models*. DEV Community. https://dev.to/kingsley/mlops-best-practices-for-deploying-machine-learning-models-4lcc

Andersen, G. (2024, February 10). *How to Build a Strong Portfolio as a Machine Learning Engineer*. Moldstud.com. https://moldstud.com/articles/p-how-to-build-a-strong-portfolio-as-a-machine-learning-engineer

Anunaya, S. (2021, August 10). *Data Preprocessing in Data Mining - A Hands on Guide*. Analytics Vidhya. https://www.analyticsvidhya.com/blog/2021/08/data-preprocessing-in-data-mining-a-hands-on-guide/

Beheshti, N. (2022, February 5). *Cross Validation and Grid Search*. Medium. https://towardsdatascience.com/cross-validation-and-grid-search-efa64b127c1b

Biswal, A. (2024, March 12). *The Complete Guide on Overfitting and Underfitting in Machine Learning*. Simplilearn.com. https://www.simplilearn.com/tutorials/machine-learning-tutorial/overfitting-and-underfitting

Buhl, N. (2023, August 9). *Mastering Data Cleaning & Data Preprocessing for Machine Learning*. Encord.com. https://encord.com/blog/data-cleaning-data-preprocessing/

Corcuera, L., Ducange, P., Marcelloni, F., Nardini, G., Noferi, A., Renda, A., Ruffini, F., Schiavo, A., Stea, G., & Virdis, A. (2023). Enabling federated learning of explainable AI models within beyond-5G/6G networks. *Computer Communications, 210*, 356–375. https://doi.org/10.1016/j.comcom.2023.07.039

DataCamp Team. (2022, December 14). *A List of the 20 Best ETL Tools and Why to Choose Them.* DataCamp. https://www.datacamp.com/blog/a-list-of-the-16-best-etl-tools-and-why-to-choose-them

Datadog. (2024, April 26). *Machine Learning Model monitoring: Best Practices.* Datadog. https://www.datadoghq.com/blog/ml-model-monitoring-in-production-best-practices/

Delua, J. (2024, May 13). *Supervised vs. Unsupervised learning: What's the difference? IBM.* https://www.ibm.com/think/topics/supervised-vs-unsupervised-learning

Ejonavi, J. (2015). *Cracking the Machine Learning interview: System Design Approaches.* Educative. https://www.educative.io/blog/cracking-machine-learning-interview-system-design

Ethan. (2024). *100+ Best ETL Tools List & Software (As of August 2024).* Portable.io. https://portable.io/learn/best-etl-tools

Serverless Architecture. (2024, April 29). GeeksforGeeks. https://www.geeksforgeeks.org/serverless-architectures/

Hardesty, L. (2019). *The history of amazon's recommendation algorithm.* Amazon Science. https://www.amazon.science/the-history-of-amazons-recommendation-algorithm

Koehrsen, W. (n.d.). *Intro to Model Tuning: Grid and Random Search.* Kaggle.com. https://www.kaggle.com/code/willkoehrsen/intro-to-model-tuning-grid-and-random-search

Krysik, A. (2024, June 14). *Netflix algorithm: How netflix uses AI to improve personalization.* Stratoflow. https://stratoflow.com/how-netflix-recommendation-algorithm-work/

Lamberti, A. (2024, March 1). *Deep Learning Model Optimization Methods.* Neptune.ai. https://neptune.ai/blog/deep-learning-model-optimization-methods

Hernandez Aros, L., Ximena, L., Gutierrez-Portela, F., Johver, J., & Samuel, M. (2024). Financial Fraud Detection through the Application of Machine Learning techniques: a Literature Review. *Humanities and Social Sciences Communications, 11*(1). https://doi.org/10.1057/s41599-024-03606-0

Nautiyal, D. (2017, November 23). *Underfitting and Overfitting in Machine Learning.* GeeksforGeeks. https://www.geeksforgeeks.org/underfitting-and-overfitting-in-machine-learning/

Nielson, V. (2023). *Model Pruning, Distillation, and Quantization, Part 1.* Deepgram. https://deepgram.com/learn/model-pruning-distillation-and-quantization-part-1

Ogunlami, A. (2023, April 26). *A hybrid approach to fraud detection*. Advancing Analytics. https://www.advancinganalytics.co.uk/blog/2023/4/21/an-hybrid-approach-to-fraud-detection

OWASP AI Security and Privacy Guide. (n.d.). Owasp. https://owasp.org/www-project-ai-security-and-privacy-guide/

Oza, N. (2024, August 2). *Attain 35% more efficiency in manufacturing with data computing*. Ace Infoway. https://www.aceinfoway.com/blog/increase-efficiency-using-data-computing

Peerdh. (2024, September 16). *Comparing Model Optimization Techniques in Tensorflow for Image Classification*. Peerdh.com. https://peerdh.com/blogs/programming-insights/comparing-model-optimization-techniques-in-tensorflow-for-image-classification

Pugh, J., Penney, L. S., Noël, P. H., Neller, S., Mader, M., Finley, E. P., Lanham, H. J., & Leykum, L. (2021). Evidence Based Processes to Prevent readmissions: More Is better, a ten-site Observational Study. *BMC Health Services Research*, *21*(1), 189. https://doi.org/10.1186/s12913-021-06193-x

What Is Data Preprocessing for Machine Learning? (n.d.). Pure Storage. https://www.purestorage.com/knowledge/what-is-data-preprocessing.html

Puri, G. (2023, November 24). What Is Interview: Meaning, Types and Formats. *Naukri's Official Blog*. https://www.naukri.com/blog/what-is-interview/

Rastogi, R. (2024, April 24). *ETL: the Ultimate Guide to Extract, Transform, Load Processes*. BuzzClan. https://buzzclan.com/data-engineering/what-is-etl/

Periyasamy, R. (2024, August 21). *ETL Best Practices*. Peliqan. https://peliqan.io/blog/etl-best-practices/

Rocco, D. (2021, May 21). *The 4 Pillars of MLOps: How to Deploy ML Models to Production*. PhData. https://www.phdata.io/blog/the-ultimate-mlops-guide-how-to-deploy-ml-models-to-production/

3.2. Tuning the hyper-parameters of an Estimator — scikit-learn 0.22 Documentation. Scikit-Learn.org. (2012). https://scikit-learn.org/stable/modules/grid_search.html

Supervised Vs Unsupervised Learning Explained. (2021, October 16). Seldon. https://www.seldon.io/supervised-vs-unsupervised-learning-explained

Data Preprocessing Techniques for Machine Learning. (2021). Slogix.in. https://slogix.in/machine-learning/data-preprocessing-techniques-for-machine-learning/

Srivastava, T. (2019, August 6). *Evaluation Metrics Machine Learning*. Analytics Vidhya. https://www.analyticsvidhya.com/blog/2019/08/11-important-model-evaluation-error-metrics/

Takyar, A. (2023, June 12). *AI Model Security*. LeewayHertz. https://www.leewayhertz.com/ai-model-security/

Team EMB. (2023, December 14). Data Preprocessing Techniques: Enhancing Model Accuracy. *EMB Blogs*. https://blog.emb.global/data-preprocessing-techniques/

Tripathy, S. S., Jafarzadegan, K., Moftakhari, H., & Moradkhani, H. (2024). Dynamic bivariate hazard forecasting of hurricanes for improved disaster preparedness. *Communications Earth & Environment, 5*(1). https://doi.org/10.1038/s43247-023-01198-2

3.2. Tuning the hyper-parameters of an Estimator — scikit-learn 0.22 Documentation. Scikit-Learn.org. (2012). https://scikit-learn.org/stable/modules/grid_search.html

Vyas, K. (2017, August 2). *Top 15 Big Data Technologies & Solutions to Watch*. Datamation. https://www.datamation.com/big-data/big-data-technologies/

Wilson, C. (2021, March 24). The Difference between Real-Time, near Real-Time & Batch Processing. *Precisely*. https://www.precisely.com/blog/big-data/difference-between-real-time-near-real-time-batch-processing-big-data

Made in the USA
Coppell, TX
16 March 2025